UNMASKING GOD

'To me, Daniel O'Leary is with Matthew, Mark, Luke and John in that he is fearless, always exploring, always confronting pain and hurt and trouble, and always finding and revealing those seeds of love and hope that shine like stars in our souls' darkness ... Daniel is a poet of God.'
— *Brendan Kennelly*

Daniel J. O'Leary

Unmasking God

REVEALING THE DIVINE IN THE ORDINARY

the columba press

in assocation with
The TABLET

First published in 2011 by
the columba press
55A Spruce Avenue, Stillorgan Industrial Park,
Blackrock, Co Dublin
in association with
THE TABLET PUBLISHING CO
1 King Street Cloisters, Clifton Walk, London W6 0QZ

Cover by Bill Bolger
Origination by The Columba Press
Printed in Ireland by Brunswick Press Ltd, Dublin

ISBN 978 1 85607 726 2

Table of Contents

Dear Reader,

Thank you for picking up this book. May it change your life. It will if you really want it to. All God needs is your 'yes'. There is an ache in everyone to be happy. But people are unaware of the great secret – that the promise and presence of joy and peace of mind is already safely within the human heart – impatiently waiting to be discovered there. That's what we mean by 'unmasking God'.

'Most people live lives of quiet desperation' wrote Thoreau. There are endless reasons for this sorry truth. In a world that suffers much disillusionment – at the failings of our religious leaders, our financial advisors, our politicians – too many have lost their joy.

There is a recurring 'absence', a sense of something missing. How do we regain the lost light, the divine nerve to welcome each new day, come what may? How do we discover a new way of being, a new way of seeing?

The excitement that pervades these pages springs from the belief that a divine power and healing is already lying within each one of us, and within all of creation. Once this revelation is taken seriously by our churches, and by ourselves, then our efforts for peace and equality, for justice and joy, will spread like wildfire.

There is another way of living our days on this troubled earth. We almost always forget (or maybe were never told) that already within us we carry the fresh wells we thirst for, the beckoning horizons for which we long, the gold hidden in the rubble of even our most dark and difficult days.

This is the core of the gospel and is at the heart of our best theology and spirituality. It is also spread over the pages of this book. It sets out to reveal 'the dearest freshness deep down things' as the poet put it. In that 'dearest' place there is no room for anxiety, guilt, shame, worry or fear anymore.

Too often religion masks God. The emphasis in these pages is about unmasking the distant God we were often told about, and restoring to our deepest centre, a warm, human, ever-forgiving Father/Mother who is helplessly in love with us. Today we need to feel the comforting presence of God in the ordinary moments of our lives.

The unmasked God is revealed, once and for all and forever, as the innermost intimacy at the heart of our daily being. God comes to us disguised as our very lives – their pain and their joy. We are called to penetrate this disguise – and to recognise God in our blossoming.

Once we try to believe in all this astonishing good news we are left with another vital question. It was asked by the poet Mary Oliver; 'What are you now planning to do with your one wild and precious life?'

God bless and lots of love,

Daniel J. O'Leary
010111

PS An earlier book *Already Within* was also a collection of my *Tablet* articles. Thank you for naming it as your favourite religious book in 2007. I dedicate this new one to you. It gives me great joy and courage when you send in your stories about discovering the new growing, healing and personal freedom that is always transforming your life (www.djoleary.com).

Spring:
The Grace of Emerging

Waiting for the ambush

Lent is often characterised as a time of self-denial for Christians, but this is not the whole story. It can be a time of extraordinary richness in which we are able to discover the limitless power of God's love.

Everything about us reaches out to be loved and to love, to become the other. We long for intimacy. We are born for it. We are drawn and driven by this original and persistent desire of our being.

Astonishingly, we are already encompassed by this ultimate and unique embrace – but we will not, dare not or cannot believe it. We risk staying stuck too long in the trappings of routine religion. Beyond our familiar 'to do' lists for Lent – the things to give up, the tasks to take on, the prayers to squeeze in, the sins to cut out – there is a deeper horizon drawing us closer into a beautiful mystery.

The pursuit of this union with God is not hampered by our imperfections and peccadilloes. The surrender to divine love is only blocked by our own futile efforts to improve, to get better, to save our souls. Beyond such mortal strivings there is a matchless immensity around the way God lures and allures our hearts with a divine determination.

When this holy ambush happens, even partially, no one is measuring merit, progress or failure any more. It is 'grace upon grace'. Astonished, we find ourselves sinking into the love that is now becoming the power and the presence, the very breath of our lives.

'Hidden with Christ in God', we care little about our standing in the hierarchies of things; we waste no sleep about what others may think of us; we are experiencing, even if only in glimpses, that unutterably sublime freedom of the children of God. Beyond creeds, formulas and rites, this deeply felt fusion with incarnate Presence reveals to us something of what falling in love with God means. In a sense, no effort is required – only the effort to let go into the pure joy of the lover's desire, to allow the love for which we were created in the first place to happen to us. We wait for our own estranged faces to find their true beauty in the radiance of God's features.

As the drop of rain assumes its full identity when surrendering to the sea, so with us. Kathleen Raine in her poem 'Message' writes:

Look, beloved child, into my eyes, see there
Your self, mirrored in that living water
From whose deep pools all images of earth are born.
See, in the gaze that holds you dear
All that you were, are and shall be for ever.

We wait for that blessed season in our lives when we empty ourselves of all that distorts the whisper of divine longing within us. All we are asked to do is to stay ready and obedient to God's fingers and lips, making new music on the silent reeds of our hearts. This astounds us. We had been told differently. The emptier we become, the more space for God to fill. The more hollow we are, the truer the music from the lips of the Flautist. In 'May I Have this Dance?' Joyce Rupp has caught the meaning:

The small wooden flute and I,
We need the one who breathes …
So that the song-starved world
May be fed with golden melodies.

At some point during one special Lent, the veils will part just enough to transfix our hearts and transform our lives. That intimate moment will happen when the divine breath blows beauty into our shape, into our face and form. Everything is affected because everything is connected. The song of Creation itself is muted when the reeds of our lives are no longer receptive to the breath of God.

'Lord only let me make my life simple and straight,' wrote Rabindranath Tagore, 'like a flute of reeds for Thee to fill with music.' The melody is pure and beautiful, new yet familiar, and it calls to us like a far wave. Our stalled heart remembers, surrenders and recognises again the melody of the Maestro. It is the music from which we come; it is the music towards which we go. We need daily silence to catch those grace notes in the cacophony of our distractedness.

Falling in love with God like this is for everyone. Human hearts are fashioned for this to happen. Nor does it mean loving the world less, and the people in it. It means we love them more. Wherever we love sensitively, passionately and faithfully, we are already in love with God. Entwined with the heart of God, our love now has no fear to it. Utterly safe, we begin to play, to thank, to bless, to live, to adore as never before.

This realisation is a daily and deeply felt transformation of our way of being and our way of seeing. We do not need to be successful, liked, praised any more; these needs are transcended. We find we can forgive almost anyone for anything; it is easier than we thought. We no longer compare, compete, complain; we do not need to. We stop judging, blaming and resenting; there is no satisfaction in doing so now. Our vision of love is deeper. 'Out beyond ideas of right and wrong there's a field,' wrote Rumi. 'I'll meet you there.'

In the still point of this bright field we come up against the edge of our darkness, the wilder frontiers of our possibilities, our passionate desire for life itself. Here in the heart of God, beyond the tyranny of a suffocating conformity, we sense the horizons for which we were created. In this silent embrace within our soul, we get younger as we grow older, we start to divine our divinity with a fiercer intent.

When we receive Holy Communion at our Lenten Mass, a transfiguration happens within us as the bread and wine die into us. Our naked souls are ravished in utter wonder. God's desire for intimacy is becoming flesh in us. Beyond words, as John Paul II once reflected, this is embodied experience. It is the ultimate lovemaking. For one shining moment of mystery we know we are 'of one being with the Father'. Delightedly it dawns on us that every moment can be like this moment. In 'All Desires Known', Janet Morley describes her experience of it:

> … and I was nothing but letting go and being held
> and there were no words and there
> needed to be no words and we flowed …
> and I was given up to the dark and
> in the darkness I was not lost
> and the wanting was like fullness and I could
> hardly hold it and I was held and
> you were dark and warm and without time and
> without words and you held me.

What's it to be?

Magnanimous or pusillanimous, the right option seems self-evident. But in life's moments of great decision the way of choice is rarely so easy or obvious.

Around this time of the liturgical season parishioners talk about how they are succeeding (or not) with their Lenten resolutions. Such preoccupations are, no doubt, useful. After decades of Lents, however, a day comes when the call is heard to begin a more challenging conversation about the state of our souls.

The conversation for me, this year, is full of tough questions about the forces that block the flow of God's life within me. Why do we mess up the inner, divine image through our shortsighted options and selfish reactions? Why do we interrupt the divine dance in our soul, forgetting the eternal incarnate rhythm? Why do we allow the fire of inner love to grow dim because our attention has strayed?

Last month I wrote here about the basic wisdom of living our lives in an unceasing surrender to God. A reader asked about how to remain in this surrendered state: how to hold and balance the flow, the fire in our lives? Surely surrender is more than a passive state of soul? It is. Once surrendered, the soul, I believe, will discern what is called 'the way of choice'. Much wisdom can be gathered from noticing the general pattern of our choices. How do you usually choose to respond to what dents your pride? Can you name the direction your choices usually take? Are you like St Paul, who chose the evil he wished to avoid? In his recent *Spe Salvi*, Pope Benedict asks us to notice how we choose 'to deceive ourselves with hidden lies'.

Michael Losier, in *Law of Attraction*, explains that we attract to our lives whatever we choose to give our best attention to, whether positive or negative. Whenever we are drawn to the need for some spring cleaning in our souls, he suggests that we first of all choose the positive horizon we wish to reach. Into this we release our energy, nourishing the vision and keeping it in focus, noticing when we allow doubts and anxieties to distract us from that horizon.

Positive and negative emotions, he writes, cannot occupy the mind at the same time. This is so significant for us. Our scriptures have always been clear that where our heart is, there will our treasure be too. Whatever is regularly going on in our mind, that is what we are attracting more of to ourselves. Our hearts, too, are creatures of habit, gradually becoming identified with the object of their hunger.

People are surprised at the extent of the choice they have about the direction of each day's living, leading to profound satisfaction or disillusion. With God's power in us, we are all blessed with the grace of choosing our way of being in the world. We do not have to be victims of what happens to us; instead, we are blessed with the power of discerning our demons as disguised occasions of grace. But we do need to keep noticing the subtle ego in our desire for control, certainty and human respect: to 'pay attention to our intention' as James Redfield puts it in *The Celestine Prophecy*.

A Cherokee leader was out in the forest initiating the young members of the tribe into adulthood. In the course of the rites he told the story about the two wolves that are always fighting in every human soul – the benevolent wolf of peace and joy, the malevolent one forever on the prowl. 'And which wolf wins?', a youngster asked. 'The one you feed', was the reply. Which wolf are we feeding with every thought, word, breath of our lives?

Thomas Aquinas asks whether, as a rule, we act out of our *anima magna*, or our *anima pusila*. The one is the option for what is generous, tending towards overlooking, letting go. The other is the habit of meanness, tending towards what is closed, negative and judgmental. It isn't about two different types of personality, more about the aspirations of each particular soul on a given day.

Imagine a horizontal line between the kinds of choices we make. At every mind's turn we are opting to move either above that line, into the light, the space, the freedom that nourishes and saves our soul: or we are going the way of wilfulness, below the line, opting for the narrow place that stifles our spirit and closes out the light. Both worlds generate a life of their own. But we grow accustomed to one. We spend most of our thinking time there. So we eventually become those thoughts. And that means that we are carrying light or darkness wherever we go.

All of this inner work is a soul-sized enterprise. To be magn-animous is a difficult habit of the heart to form. To keep substit-uting the blaming, resentful thought for the liberating one is truly the work of the saint. It is a spiritual skill to pause – for the brevity of a breath or the long season of a deeper sorrow – to find that space of choice, so as to discern and purify the motiv-ation behind our response.

To be big enough to overlook many things, to let go of resent-ment over minor annoyances and hurts, can seem an impossible task. Even to begin to explore the suppressed and graceless neg-ativities that lie buried beneath the veneer of our public roles and rituals is a rare and daunting moment of conversion.

There is something pitifully seductive about the way our wayward minds keep returning to pick over the poisoned meat of resentment and revenge. Vigilance is needed to break that deadly habit, happening just below the level of our awareness. We make space for the grace to choose when we walk away from the look, the word, the thought that could hold us captive for the rest of that day. When, without looking back, we trans-form that moment into a kind of blessing, then we are experienc-ing the meaning of being redeemed.

Choosing, first in many smaller ways, to let go of resentment, anxiety and of all victim roles, while there is still time, is the only way to prepare for the final choices of our ultimate destiny. Viktor Frankl, purified in the crucifixion of his concentration camp experiences, rejoiced in what he called 'the final freedom' – the freedom to choose to love the one who was intent on de-stroying his life.

Lent is about choices. Jesus himself was familiar with that sacred space, the space between refusing and accepting the chalices of-fered by his Father during his brief life. On his Cross, he chose to forgive his enemies, to even love them. And later, at the moment of his death, after an intense struggle with his terrible doubt, Jesus uttered his whispered 'yes' to his beloved Father before his soul left him.

Our most important life choices are rarely obvious or easy. Side by side, they look alike, and often live at the same address. A friend of mine wears a small dark heart and a small bright one on her necklace. John O'Donohue hoped that at the hour of our death, when we find that through fear or frailty we chose the 'wrong' path, in God's astonishing love, the untaken choice, the unlived destiny, is still offered as an open possibility.

Gold in the dust

It's hard to be good, and human beings are repeat offenders. Yet the ashes that mark foreheads on Ash Wednesday are a reminder not only of sin, and of the state to which we will return, but of the extraordinary paradoxes at the heart of the Christian faith.

I remember it like yesterday. My first temptation. It happened halfway through Lent in the year of my first Holy Communion. 'Mammy, Mammy,' I wailed, 'I've committed a sin.' I was clutching an old cake tin full of all the humbugs, jelly babies and pear drops that I had given up for Lent. It was a bizarre bargain. I would give them up for God if I could still save them up for an Easter Sunday orgy!

By now the bull's eyes, the dolly mixtures, the pieces of Killarney sticks of rock, were all a horrible sticky mess because I took the tin around everywhere with me just to be sure, and kept opening it every few minutes to smell, stare and touch in the most pathetic and revolting manner. After my confession no words of blame came from my mother's lips. They never did. 'Being good is hard, Dan,' she said, 'and it takes a long time to be good.'

It was probably her gentle way of saying, 'Remember, little man, you are only dust.' There isn't much you can do about dust to change its image. It is the graphic symbol of nothingness, of powerlessness, of anonymous insignificance. Scripture insists we are dust. We are always in the process of dying. From the moment of our birth, our sails are inexorably set for the flat, obscured shoreline of death.

Nor does Lent call us away from this depressing scenario of our finite ordinariness. It is the raw reminder of it – of the dust we came from, and to which we will return. To be a follower of the Lenten Jesus is to be convinced again and again that we are creatures of pain and weakness, continually losing our bearings in the voyage of our lives. And until we know ourselves to be lost we can never be found.

Next Wednesday we will again be given a sober appraisal of the context of our existence. That context is dust. And there are no exceptions. Much as we try to fudge it, to wriggle away from it, even to deny it, Jesus, too, was alarmingly human – and remains that way in heaven to this very day. And his wounds still bleed there.

There is no escape from the human condition. Yet that is the condition which God cannot resist. It is the very condition in which God chose to be revealed! We get to heaven, then, not by avoiding or denying the dust around and within us, but by completely entering into that darkened state. It is in our dust that we are saved. 'The Word became dust.' This is another way of asserting, our scriptural scholars assure us, that 'The Word became flesh'.

That is the key which unlocks impossible doors. It is the 'hinge', as Tertullian puts it, 'on which salvation turns'. Since the Incarnation, dust and flesh designate not only the hinge and pivot of the movement into nothingness and death, but also the hinge and pivot of a movement that passes through dust and death into the eternity of God.

In his reflections on Lent, Karl Rahner wrote: 'The downward motion of the believer, the descent with Christ into the dust of the earth, has become an upward motion, an ascent above the highest heaven. Christianity does not set us free from the flesh and dust, nor does it bypass flesh and dust; it goes right through flesh and dust. And that is why the expression 'you are dust' is still applicable to us; rightly understood, it is a complete expression of life.'

Julian of Norwich believed that God will even use our sins to transform us. 'Sin shall not be a shame to humans, but a glory ... The mark of sin shall be turned to honour.' True recognition of our basic nothingness, or, as Karl Barth put it, of our 'groundlessness', is a humbling experience, but it forces us to trust in unconditional love. 'That's what I work with,' God says. 'That's all I can ever work with!' It is with the flawed seed, the damaged beauty, that God does great things.

Henri Nouwen was well aware of the complicated ambiguity of life. He himself was only too familiar with the dust of the human condition – in his own unhappiness, his pettiness, his neediness, his fear.

'There's dust everywhere,' he wrote. 'It seems that there is no such thing as a clearcut, pure joy. In every satisfaction there is an awareness of limitations. In every success there is the fear of jealousy. In every embrace there is loneliness. But this intimate experience in which every bit of life is touched by a bit of death, can point us beyond the limits of our existence.'

Thomas Merton's famous epiphany on the corner of Walnut and 4th Streets in Louisville, Kentucky, happened in a very ordinary shopping area. 'It is a glorious destiny to be a member of the human race, though it is a race dedicated to so many absurdities, sorrows, stupidities, and one which makes many terrible mistakes: yet, with all that, God himself gloried in becoming a member of the human race.'

This much lionised contemplative surprised many by revealing himself as 'noisy, full of the racket of imperfections and passions and the wide-open wounds left by sin, full of faults and envies and miseries, full of my own intolerable emptiness.' The hidden revelation of Lent is that the gate to God is everywhere: and that it swings most splendidly in every particle of the dust of our lives.

On Wednesday the priest will trace a cross of ashes on us and tell us again that we are dust. If we only knew, these are the best words we will ever hear. They remind us, because we are sisters and brothers of the incarnate Lord who became dust for us, that in our nothingness, too, we are filled with eternity, in our futility we are redeemed, and in our sin-strewn lives we are showered with the hidden graces of true glory.

To say this is easy. To suffer it is hard. Rahner is so accurate in describing the boredom of everyday routine, the disappointments that we experience in everything – in ourselves, in our neighbours, in the church. We lose heart, he said, 'in the anxiety of our days, in the futility of our work, in the brutal harshness of our splintered world', and in the wretched tins of humbugs we cannot resist. Again and again we shall lie in the dust of our failures, humiliated and wanting to cry.

And yet, and yet, on each Ash Wednesday, our church faithfully reminds us that we are walking sacraments of Christian paradox. Outwardly we carry the grey cross of nothingness on our foreheads: inwardly our hearts believe that everything is already ours. Outwardly we weep and bleed as we stumble up the grimy Calvary of our lives; inwardly our dust is already shining with Easter gold.

Human touch of Easter

With Holy Week ahead of us, we should reflect on the full humanity of God, whose power, presence and promise can now and for all time come to us in a form and expression we can understand, and with whom we can be one.

My spondylosis was flaring up again and needed attention. The surgery waiting-room was hot and crowded. A child with some kind of painful rash was becoming alarmingly upset. The flustered mother was holding a baby in her lap. She pleaded with, explained to, and scolded the suffering, obstreperous little girl to no avail. We were all becoming uneasy. Clearly embarrassed, the mother handed her baby to the concerned woman next to her and reached for her inconsolable child. She lifted her high, and held her firmly against her breast. We all waited. After a few seconds a sweet silence descended on the room.

Easter, I think, is a bit like that. It reminds us that God reaches us in human touch. It is in our physical, earthy humanity that we heal and save each other. We have learned this from a human God. John placed his ear on the heart of Jesus at the Last Supper. Mary Magdalene touched his feet, Thomas his wounds. Tertullian, a very early Church Father, in an untranslatable play on words, put it all very succinctly when he said *caro cardo salutis* – it is in the flesh that salvation hinges.

And the mystery has a relevance beyond human beings alone. Since God became human in Jesus, a becoming that exploded forth at Easter, we are called to believe that not only the human condition but the earth itself from which it springs are the real presence of God's own essence. At his poetic best, John Paul II repeatedly and delightedly kept reminding us of this 'cosmic' picture.

From the beginning we have been too slow to believe the astonishing reality of Incarnation. The power, presence and promise of God are now accessible in the form and expression of our humanity, within its dreams, relationships, emotions and all its experiences. They are also inextricably intertwined with the fabric and core of the world itself. We forever struggle with the challenging truth that in the fleshing of the Word, and in the raising of that same Word, God discarded divine immunity. For all time, God wished to be known as the Human One with the five senses, the Son of Man, who is now delighted to be confined, unprotected, within the constraints of the finite realities of a beloved world.

Like the Incarnation itself, Easter too is about bodies, personal and cosmic. The true orthodoxy of Catholic Christianity has never deviated from this teaching. What is to be avoided is a view that sees Jesus taking a solo flight back to the shores of heaven on that Paschal morning. There is no sacramentality in such a misunderstanding. Neither is it only a question of a personal salvation for our individual souls. The truth of Resurrection, revealed at Easter, is that in our present, frail and redeemed bodies, we carry the saving power of God. The risen Christ is the eternal sacrament of a risen humanity and a risen world.

When we pay attention we notice this incarnate, compassionate presence all around us. Even as I write these very words a neighbour, on the way back from the surgery, called in for a chat. She happened to mention that our local doctor, a Hindu, had, with his wife, decided to sell their belongings here so as to work in a small African village later this year. They plan to stay there for the rest of their lives. Having worked in the village last summer, they had, they said, no choice. God has no favourites.

Ahead of us lies Holy Week. Emphasised throughout its days is the persistent reality of the full humanity of God. The movement from death to life, from darkness to light, identifiable in every phase of the liturgy, is remembered in flesh, tears, blood – all the emotions of a very human being. And by virtue of our solidarity with the Saviour, everyone and everything is redeemed and completed, and, from the inside out, the world itself is renewed and restored.

In our celebrating of the Paschal mystery maybe we skip too quickly from Good Friday to the Easter Vigil. It is Holy Saturday, silent and empty, that holds the vital key which includes us, human beings, at the heart of Easter. It is the timeless moment when we, at our lowest, are sought and found by Jesus. Having descended to the very womb of the earth, he gave the earth his divine life forever. This is the new creation of a transfigured earth into which, not out of which, Christ died and was raised. At its inner core, the world is now transformed. It is a world in which everything belongs. In a short while we will be celebrating the intrinsic unity of the cosmic, the human and the divine – a unity which began in God's imagination before the world began. We will struggle with this truth.

The dualistic virus that has infected the ecclesiastical system over the centuries has great difficulty in believing the truth of seeing the presence of the risen Christ in the most ordinary and 'secular' places. It has great trouble, in fact, in believing what the Incarnation reveals about the divine value of all Creation and all lived lives. There is a chilling edge to ecclesiastical references to 'our Godless' lives, society or world – the very places that God, named or not, is utterly delighted to inhabit. Christ is risen because in death he redeemed for ever the deepest parts of all human hearts, the innermost centre of all earthly existence, where he is pleased to live.

Karl Rahner writes: 'What we call his resurrection – and unthinkingly take to be his own private destiny – is only the first surface indication that all reality has already changed in the really decisive depth of things. The new creation has already started, the new power of a transfigured earth is already being formed from the world's innermost heart, into which Christ has descended by dying … He is here. He is the heart of this earthly world and the mysterious seal of its eternal validity.'

Jesus did not begin to save the world by transfiguring first the visible symptoms. Because the evil of injustice, war and greed still carves new marks in the face of the earth, we fear that Easter really is about the next life. We wonder whether the world is absolutely saved. But, as with sick and shallow institutions and churches, the resistant surface is usually the last to collapse. Easter faith is about believing in the light while it is still dark. The Triduum is never over. And a vital contribution still belongs to us.

Much dying to self is demanded so as to complete in our time what Jesus achieved once and for all at that first Passover. What remains now is that risen love should burst forth from the grave of our own hearts. Divine energy must rise from the core of our being. We are not saved from the world, we are saved for the world; made whole again so as to be reconcilers and peacemakers for humanity and for the earth itself. It has already happened once for all in history; only we can make sure it is happening today.

Open your eyes

When we love someone, we draw out the beauty that is within them, our tenderness persuading their true loveliness to emerge. Similarly at Easter, falsehood melts away and things appear as they really are.

A friend of mine entered for last year's *Britain's Got Talent* auditions. I tuned in to one of the first episodes. The panel judges were finding it all rather boring and predictable. During the interval they said so. Paul Potts, a sad-faced young man from Wales, was next up. He said he would like to be an opera singer. I noticed two of the three judges throwing cynical glances at each other. Then Paul opened his mouth, and a voice of power and beauty soared through the auditorium, capturing our hearts.

Paul went on to win the national competition and to reveal a talent worthy of any of the 'three tenors' themselves. At the Royal Variety Performance before the year ended, the three chastened judges more or less publicly apologised to Paul, who was performing that night. In the beginning, they were looking at him, but they had not 'seen' him. They had forgotten that people do not see things as they are; they see things as *they* are. But now their eyes were opened. They finally saw the real Paul Potts.

I have long wondered why the risen Jesus was unrecognised by Mary and the disciples. But something clicked in my heart as I recently listened to the Dominican Timothy Radcliffe. It wasn't, he said, that they knew Jesus before and did not recognise him now. It was more that they never really knew him, or rather, as Herbert McCabe put it, 'they thought they knew him', and now they were meeting the real Jesus as if for the first time. The miracle of Easter was already opening their eyes. The blindfold preventing them from fully recognising him before was now being removed. Love was bringing clear vision. It was transforming the blurred, the false; it was revealing the real, the beautiful. For one bright moment they glimpsed pure truth.

In one of John O'Donohue's last poems he speaks to the mother of a young criminal:

No one else can see beauty in his darkened life now.
His image has closed

Like a shadow.
But he is yours;
And you have different eyes
That hold his yesterdays
In pictures no one else remembers.
He is yours in a way no words could ever tell;
And you can see through the stranger this deed has made him
And still find the countenance of your son.

The gift of true seeing has always been at the heart of Christianity. Easter is about taking away rather than about adding on; more about subtraction than addition; more about unblocking than increasing. It happened to those on the road to Emmaus. Pope Benedict in *Spe Salvi* writes, 'Before [the risen Christ's] gaze all falsehood melts away ... The holy power of his love sears through us like a flame.' No wonder their hearts burned within them. And then, before their very eyes, the fierce invincibility and utter vulnerability of our human God were constellated in a fistful of bread on the rough surface of a stained table in a country inn.

Easter is the death of illusion, the window of recognition, the work of restoration. Redemption is the clear courageous vision of what happens, of what is. Too often, in our fear of naked 'is-ness', we shrink from it. While we are created for truth we cannot bear too much reality! 'We would rather be ruined than changed,' wrote W. H. Auden. 'We would rather die in our dread than climb the cross of the moment and see our illusions die.' Thus, as Francis Thompson knew, 'with our estranged eyes we miss the many-splendoured thing.'

'Something prevented them from recognising him.' What a striking way of putting it. Maybe the 'thing' that prevented them wasn't a thing at all. Maybe it was an absence that still blinded them – the absence of a fully purified vision. Love fills in the gaps and heals the flaws. It sees perfection from within, the beauty already there. We call it the sacrament of presence – of real presence.

A young monk was returning to the monastery after his annual retreat. Waiting for him was the older monk who always criticised him, belittled him. 'Out skiving again,' the young

monk was cuttingly greeted, 'and in spite of all your costly retreats you still look no different to me.' The young monk
paused, smiled a small smile and murmured, 'Ah, maybe; but
you look different to me.'

A few weeks ago the theologian Gerald O'Collins told a
group of us a story about the journalist who was picking his
way, at dawn, along the severely bombed streets of Second
World War London. The smoke and smell of the previous
night's devastation still hung heavily in the air. A young woman
emerged from a blacked-out flat. 'Terrible night!' he called out.
'Yes,' she smiled, cradling her wide-eyed baby, 'but what a wonderful morning.'

Only love can catch the truth. The hidden Christ, in the sight-
less tomb, had embraced and transformed all that blurs and
blinds. Everything around him that morning was epiphany. It
was about recognition. What was until then partially perceived
now found its fullest definition. Those who loved and suffered
most recognised him first – the beloved disciples John and Mary.

Only with the painfully purified heart do we see rightly.
There is an apprenticeship to the vision of love. The disciples
heading for Emmaus had to learn the steps. So must we. To be
sure, it is gift. But gift, like surprise, favours the prepared heart.
First, the wise one counselled, try to see and love a stone. Then
try to truly see and love a cloud. Wait a while and begin to love a
petal, a bird, a star; and then, and only then, try to see and love a
human being. 'Christ,' Thomas Aquinas insisted, 'is rising.'

Anything, anywhere, any time can be the beginning of this
apprenticeship into the really real. Nothing is too insignificant
to be an epiphany of eternity. And when it happens, like the first
Easter, it stays forever. 'You must know,' wrote John Paul II,
'that there is no return from this vision.' In 'Memory', Thomas
Aldrich writes about the moment the eyes of his heart were
blessed with true sight:

> My mind lets go a thousand things,
> Like dates of wars and deaths of kings,
> And yet recalls the very hour –
> 'Twas noon by yonder village tower,
> and on the last blue noon in May –
> the wind came briskly up this way,

crisping the brook beside the road;
then, pausing here, let down its load
of pine-scents, and shook listlessly
two petals from that wild-rose tree.

From man's man to free man

A visit to a male prison revealed the damage that has been done to so many young men, some serving jail sentences, but most imprisoned in other ways. Yet the painful path to true liberation, through death to life, was also pointed out.

Late-in-the-season snow was tumbling down as I drove through the silent streets of a Yorkshire city on Easter Sunday morning. It was a great privilege to celebrate Mass with a group of men in one of HM Prisons. The experience affected me deeply. The truth of the Triduum had weakened the walls of my usual professional defences.

The greatest fear of most public figures, some piece of research claims, is the fear of being found out. And so many of us, 'on the outside', pretend, pull rank and deny when our misdemeanors and mistakes come under scrutiny.

But these men had nowhere to hide. Lined up, dressed down, watched, they seemed anguished, shamed. They sat there as though naked. This struck me particularly poignantly. They were found out, and found guilty, and they just had to spend each long day in their own private purgatory of pain.

Interspersed among the 50 or so men were four women. They were there as chaplains and their assistants. Their presence was striking. There was a kind of harmony and acceptance between them all that could be sensed. Full of firmness, respect and compassion before these self-conscious, vulnerable men, they were sensitive companions, restoring some semblance of self-esteem and self-belief to broken psyches. Whatever male and female energy may mean, they seemed to me to be woven together uniquely that special morning.

I began to wonder how this prison could be a place of grace for those men. Where to begin? 'In the desert of the heart, let the healing fountain start.' Could the waters of self-forgiveness spring from here? How, I wondered, would the women prepare those men for a death, for a new birth? 'Unless the grain of wheat dies . . .' How would they convince them of the need for a painful planting, a slow gestation through an inner dying. How were these men ever going to bless their deserted partners with a new-found insight, or teach their children the hidden harvest of a damaged life? Even for Jesus, it took a long time for his wounds to reveal their wisdom.

It is never easy to face your demons, often impulsive and violent. It is more difficult still to share these burning emotions with others. To be vulnerable in this way is against everything that male machismo stands for. Unbidden, an innate sense of competition seems to spring up whenever men gather together. Behind the masks of a confident bravado lies a constant fear of failure, a struggling sense of self-worth.

A key issue for most men is the nature of their relationships with their fathers. The father-son relationship is at the heart of the holistic growing and maturing of the boy, the young man, the middle-aged man. Self-aware men feel the negative effects on their lives of their 'absent fathers'. Jesus knew something about this abandonment, too, we were reminded on Good Friday. These relationships, present and absent, can carry the deepest trauma. Unless this reality is acknowledged and given healing space, it can make a full life impossible.

As I chatted with a few of the prisoners that morning I sensed in them a tentative searching for a lost self, for a fresh beginning. Some seemed able to accept the hard reality of their situation. It was an infectious kind of common culpability, a moment of innocence almost, that I felt drawn into. How strange that such are the times, and such are the places, all marked by male brokenness and loss, when one is conscious of a deep sense of healing! In the oddest way, among them, I felt forgiven.

There is an increasing need, acknowledged or not, among men, for spiritual direction and for what is called 'inner work'. There is a male spirituality that is nurtured and fostered at men's 'rights of passage' sessions. These increasingly popular gatherings encourage a stripping of masks so as to let go of illusions, to feel the pain of humiliation, to discern the truth in a male world so often full of half-lies. This kind of difficult honesty reveals many conditions that keep men stuck in their maturing. Sibling and peer rivalry, subtle fear of inadequacy on a number of fronts, suppressed grief, an overwhelming pressure to 'prove oneself' before father and significant others, are all among the pressing causes of anger, depression, addiction and despair among men, including fellow priests.

Fr Richard Rohr, OFM, a master teacher, believes that until men can face their own demons and death, in reality or in ritual, they will continue to be driven by the relentless demands of the ego, stuck and obsessed with the interests and habits of the first decades of life. There must be a difficult transforming death before a new horizon opens us. Without a hard-won awareness, a kind of second birth, men will always tend to abuse power and people, to remain trapped in closed and costly competitions and compulsions.

Throughout these sessions, men are helped to mature through an awareness of the midlife turning point between the ascendant, driven, upward thrust of our careers and the more selective, generative and looser tempo of descent in our final decades. Missing this vital turning drives us down many deadly culs-de-sac.

I spent a 'men's week' with Fr Richard and 80 others at Ghost Ranch in the high sierras of a New Mexico desert. It was a painful and liberating experience, a raw ritual of passage that reached personal and painful places normally untouched by our liturgical celebrations. It was about the death of the false self, the cherishing of the true self. Priests and lay folk wept at their damaged lives, at the unwitting abuses they were suffering in their controlling environments; we were glad at the new freedom we were finding, risking the recovery of our God-given selves, and telling the truth once more.

It was a kind of Passover experience. All our wounds were becoming sacred wounds. We were experiencing, through the grace of grief, a transformation into authenticity. We had a hard time of it finding our souls; there is a heavy cost for such discipleship. We were losing much; we were gaining more. Because we felt held by God we did not need to worry about the details of the future.

Such a pilgrim is walking with his wound. He is giving all else away. He has nothing. And yet, as Fr Richard said to us on the final day, holding high the broken, nourishing bread of a wounded life on a canyon-rim of stunning beauty, 'he has it all'.

Divinely human

The explosive power of God lies in the radical nature of Jesus and his taking on of the three great sufferings of physical pain, the loss of his good name and a sense of ultimate abandonment. To deny his humanity is to deny salvation.

A sudden summons from the bishop startles most priests. It certainly startled me some decades ago when, in my first parish, the ominous call came. In the Sixties, newly ordained priests were required to send in their homily notes for scrutiny by the bishop. Those endless moments in the waiting room will never leave my mind. Rifling through my handwritten pages, the bishop beckoned me into his office, put on his glasses, smiled grimly and said: 'Sit down, Fr O'Leary. After reading your homily for the first Sunday in Lent, I'm left with no option but to conclude that you really believe that Jesus was actually tempted to sin.'

Much human versus divine water has flowed under the bridges of ecclesiastical debate since those days. It still does. One thing is sure – whichever way the age-old argument goes, there can be no denying the utter, radical humanity of Jesus. His absolute humanity is, by its very defined and intrinsic meaning, the key to the understanding of the mystery of our redemption. Outside the flesh there's no salvation. Moreover, anything that diminishes our belief in the true humanity of Jesus diminishes our belief in the truth of our own humanity. It is impossible to portray Jesus as being *too* human.

Jesus was so thoroughly human that he scandalised his neighbours more than once. He came eating and drinking and they called him a glutton and a drunkard. He showed his frustration and his impatience, his profound need for male and female company. He took on the three great sufferings of physical pain, the loss of his good name, and a sense of ultimate abandonment by his father. He was courageous only because he was no stranger to fear, and he confronted both the evil around him and in the demons of his own soul. He grew in wisdom and age and grace.

Just as it was the humanity of Jesus that attracted people to him, so it is with us priests. It is our vulnerable humanity as servant-priests that people can identify with – not our clerical strength.

And just as Jesus had to enter into the desert of his own heart, and face his own temptations (and, *pace* the bishop, they were real!), so too with the clergy.

'The fundamental witness of the priest,' said Archbishop Diarmuid Martin, 'will always be the authenticity of his own life.' This, in the end, is what reveals God's compassion and saves the world. 'The challenge,' said Bishop Donal Murray, 'is to humanise the world we live in. People revere that which is closest to the human heart.'

Giving retreats to priests is a wonderful (and challenging) experience. Frequently at a low ebb, they desperately struggle to save their morale, their sanity, their faith, their lives. Only at privileged times and in secure places does the truth of their inner battles of the soul emerge – battles of belief, battles of addiction, battles of personal survival. Invariably our group-sharing leads us to explore the mystery of our humanity. This is the hub around which everything else revolves. The malaise of priesthood will never be healed by top-down discussions around magisterial directives and institutional roles. It will only be engaged, and transcended, by returning to, and nourishing, the messy, needy heart of our common humanity.

How else could we live with our secret desires and weaknesses if we did not believe that, through their assumption by Jesus, they are now transformed? Would we ever tell the truth in our preaching, sometimes at significant personal cost, if Jesus had not overcome his own fear of others, and spoken honestly from his convictions? How could we cope with the betrayal, deceit and draining disappointment in our lives if we were not convinced that they played an intrinsic part in the life of Jesus, before us, and are therefore redeemed? How would we live with the loss, loneliness and quiet desperation that haunt our days and nights if we ever doubted that they were constant visitors during the days and nights of Jesus as well? And how would we ever keep struggling for liberation where injustice is rampant if we doubted that the divinity of Jesus is most clearly revealed in his own broken and marginalised humanity?

God's explosive power lies in the humanity of Jesus – and therefore of all of us. When that truth goes out of focus, the true vision of God's self-gift is blurred. Something vital for our hope is missing. Very often it is only when unwillingly vulnerable, and hanging on the ropes of our pain, that we, as priests, begin to understand the necessity of that unalterable and astonishing revelation.

Any mindset that sees the divinity and humanity of Jesus as 'over-against' each other, as competing realities within his person, undermines and even removes the indispensable basis of our salvation. Put another way, whenever the incarnate and intrinsic unity of the human and divine in Jesus is misunderstood or denied, a pervasive dualism will falsely separate God from where God wants to be, and is delighted to be found – that is, in the very imperfection and poverty of our wild, wayward and wonderful lives. There is little room for manoeuvre in the clear assertion of *Gaudium et Spes*: '[Jesus] worked with human hands, thought with a human mind, acted by human choice, and loved with a human heart. He has truly been made one of us ...' For the Christian, the divinity of Christ will ever be inseparable from his humanity. Divinity, in fact, is fully realised humanity.

If Jesus had not somehow taken on himself the agonies and ecstasies of our lives, the extremes of pride, prejudice and passion, then all would not have been saved. *Quod non assumptus, non redemptus*. There is a profound and current threat to the developing and spreading of this original and greening vision. A blind and fearful clericalism, still caught in a fatal misunderstanding of the doctrine of the Fall, strikes at the heart of the beautiful revelation of the Incarnation. This mindset is uncomfortable with, and suspicious of, authentic humanity. 'Do we replace our humanity,' asks Bishop Brian Noble, 'by an inhuman clericalism?'

Pope John Paul II has left us a gem of wisdom to ponder on. 'What the world needs today,' he wrote, 'are ministers of the gospel who are experts in humanity, who have a profound awareness of the hearts of present-day men and women, participating in their joys and hopes, anguish and sadness, and who are at the same time contemplatives who have fallen in love with God. For this we need new saints.'

Find your own Calcutta

In preparing to commemorate the Resurrection, we should, rather than pursue a private line to God, be asking some very public questions about our personal life choices, such as what we buy, how we vote, how simply we live, our sense of solidarity with others.

Cusco, city of the Inca gods, is perched on a plateau of the Peruvian Andes. The people of the city, ever ready to party, will soon be celebrating Easter with gusto. They are famous for it. Huacaypata, Cusco's square, is always full of vibrant colour and the sound of music.

But in South America I also discovered a less glamorous reality – the poverty of these same people that is more in tune with Lenten fasting than Easter rejoicing. I stayed with the Missionary Society of St James the Apostle, a group of priests from England, Ireland and the United States that endeavours to build basic communities of compassion among the destitute families in the slums and deserts of their huge parishes in Ecuador and Peru. It is another way, I discovered, of being a church.

The priests I have met out here are worried about the exploitation of the natural resources, the quality of life, the building of self-respect, the restoring of a voice to voiceless people. They are clearly not impressed by what they called 'a telephone spirituality' – me and God on a private line where I can save my soul without leaving the house. Their mission statement, rather, is about identifying the ways we are called to complete the Passover of Jesus in the relentless pursuit of justice and freedom for every person and for creation itself.

In Lima I met Fr Peter, an Irish Columban theologian. He spoke about institutional sin, cultural violence, the unity of history, the need for water and the threat of climate change. These are the issues at the heart of the shanty towns of South America, and in Africa, India and across the world. They are central to the core of gospel values too.

While I was there, Gustavo Gutierrez, the champion of liberation theology, gave a seminar on 'the human face of Jesus; the divine face of humanity'. This title tells it all. Trapped behind the bars of utter powerlessness (but with limitless potential for development), impoverished people are witnesses, as Pope

Benedict emphasised in Brazil in 2007, of the essence of God's presence. For them, Resurrection carries a very earthy and practical context. There is always the temptation to shrink and spiritualise the horizons of Matthew 25. For those who are trapped in the tightening net of a merciless exploitation, Easter must be a liberating experience to be lived before it becomes a liturgy to be celebrated.

I left Lima with uneasy thoughts. To what extent have we in the West grasped the naked truth revealed by a God who was fleshed into the condition of oppression and persecution? And do we still substitute membership of an institution for the painful personal and communal dying which is the only way to establish and purify the Kingdom of God on earth? For whom, in all honesty, is our preferential option made?

It is almost impossible for many of us to appreciate the implications of this essential Christian teaching about the divine presence in a deprived humanity, about the conviction that every man, woman and child is uniquely precious, equal and blessed. The consequences of such a belief are shattering, for it calls into question our attitudes towards our society, for instance its military, political, economic and social policies that are considered reasonable by so many of us today. It also asks us hard questions about the practical life choices we make daily – what we buy, how we vote, how simply we live, our sense of solidarity with others. For the Christian, St John Chrysostom puts it another way: 'Do you wish to honour the body of Christ? Do not ignore him when he is naked. Do not pay him homage in the temple clad in silk, only to neglect him outside when he is ill-clad. What good is it if the eucharistic table is overloaded with golden chalices when your brother is dying of hunger? Start by satisfying his hunger and then, with what is left over, you may adorn the altar as well.'

Many Lenten readings focus on the challenging realities of Jesus' humanity – God in the distressing disguise of the anguished *anawim*: the poor of the Lord. Only within the flawed flesh does redemption happen. There is no other place for healing and hurt to meet, for grace and sin to embrace, for a damaged beauty to be restored. Salvation is crafted in the workshops of poor people's lives and rich people's greed. It is extraordinary how often, in our originally sinful myopia, we mistake a universal call to save the world for the private pursuit of individual bliss in heaven.

There is another profound point to be emphasised in co-creating a better world with God. We do not all need to become missionaries in faraway places. 'Find your own Calcutta,' Mother Teresa said to those who complained that India was too far away. There are many shanty-town kingdoms to be built around us, wherever we live, beginning with the one in our own heart. It is not about doing great things in foreign lands, she said, but about doing ordinary things with great love. This is what the murdered martyr Oscar Romero wrote: 'How beautiful will be the day when all the baptised understand that their job is a priestly work, that just as I celebrate Mass at this altar, so each carpenter celebrates Mass at his workbench, and each metalworker, each professional, each doctor with the scalpel, the market woman at her stand, is performing a priestly office!'

The French contemplative and activist Madeleine Delbrel wanted to live without any hint of dualism between holy insiders and outsiders, between the religious and the profane. She brought a whole new face to the work of evangelising. 'Each tiny act is an extraordinary event, she wrote in *We, the Ordinary People of the Streets*, 'in which heaven is given to us, in which we can give heaven to others. Whatever it is – the telephone that rings, the bus that's late, the headache or toothache, the conversations that spring up, the knock on the door – they are all the outer shell (the sacrament) of an amazing inner reality, the soul's encounter with God's beautiful grace.' It takes a great love, and many deaths, to transform the eyes of our soul so as to see God's face in every face. And inevitably, inexorably, this love, this hope, will lead to a crucifixion.

Still echoing in my heart as we approach Holy Week is Romero's mighty paean to the Risen Christ – a personal *Exultet* that keeps a light in the eyes of those I visited in Peru. Two weeks before his assassination, and clearly anticipating his fate, he exclaimed in his final interview: 'I do not believe in death but in the Resurrection. If they kill me, I shall rise again in the Salvadoran people.'

A delight in company

For many parishioners, God remains a punitive figure, chalking up sins to be punished. Here, a parish priest describes how his rediscovery of a simpler theology of nature and grace, with God grounded in the ordinariness of people's lives, transformed his mission.

The cherry tree was asked, 'Speak to us of God,' and the cherry tree blossomed! My life as a priest was transformed when I began to believe that God was a lover with a passion for the healing and blossoming of all people, of all Creation.

After decades of clerical ministry I began to realise that what people were yearning for, much more than information about the church and its doctrines, was the actual redeeming reassurance of God in their daily lives. They wanted the experience of God more than knowledge about him. They longed for, in the here and now, light in their darkness, hope in their despair, courage in their fear.

This insight into the true meaning of Incarnation became the motivating driving force of my ministry. It was the touch of the real presence of God in their lived lives that people wanted to feel. To be told each Sunday about the utter holiness of their families was the good news that they waited to hear. They so sorely needed to be reassured that they are extravagantly and unconditionally loved by a most beautiful God.

The rediscovery of this orthodox (but mostly forgotten) theology of nature and grace transformed my consciousness of the mystery of the Incarnation, of the humanising of God. The whole enterprise and privilege of being a priest took on a radically new meaning. My work was less about routine maintenance and more about the enrichment of each one's creativity and sense of self: less about playing a clerical role in an institutional church and more about human compassion and service.

It takes time for the bleak picture of a God who punishes, and remembers sins, to be transformed into a God who delights in being one of us. 'God is sheer joy', wrote St Thomas Aquinas, 'and sheer joy demands company.' This astonishing revelation throws up huge challenges for those familiar only with a radically misunderstood theology of fall and redemption. Sin or no sin, it was always God's passionate desire to become just like us.

As a priest, I saw myself as a kind of midwife – a midwife of the sacredness already within the parishioners in the ordinariness of their days, in the routines of their relationships, in the high and low points of their precious days. Everything about them was grace-filled – when they encouraged each other, when they forgave each other, when they loved each other. This was God in action. I was the prism to help them perceive this, to see their true colours uniquely shining from the weekdays of their lives.

Alive within our churches there is still a deadly and deep-seated dualism dividing the holy from the human. Even though that dichotomy was definitively ended the night that God became human, the body of the church is still infected with the debilitating virus. The sacraments we celebrate in our parishes are celebrations of the holiness already within our lives – in the joy of a new birth, in the pain of our darkness, in the holiness of human love, in the desires of our hearts, in reconciliation with the wider community, in the dream of the earth.

All of this led to a shift in the way that church communities evolved. It is all about calling out the inner gifts of everyone, the encouraging of people to see themselves as made in God's image. We are God's delight. It is about helping people understand that the inner conversion of their hearts was what Jesus was after, not just the improved religious observation or increased church attendance that we often mistake for inner transformation.

For myself this perspective makes me feel a priest now more than ever before. I have felt called to help parishioners to look at life with the sacramental vision – a way of seeing that recognises God's face in every face, a God who comes to us disguised as life. It has been written on their hearts from the very beginning. This vision of God's reign among us has increased our sensitivity to issues of justice everywhere, to the care of the earth, to engage with the destruction and exploitation caused by human greed. In a pluralist world that is moving so swiftly – with its powerful drives for good and evil, its sounds of glory and cries of despair – an incarnational faith based on the goodness of creation, and of each human being, is truly timely. Parishioners can then be filled with a sense of their own responsibility for healing brokenness – within their communities and in the world. But first it has to happen within their hearts.

As I came to realise all this as a parish priest, pastoral ministries became collaborative. With minds, hearts and bodies we studied, worked and prayed. The inner journey preceded the outer one. We were often inspired by these words of Pope John Paul II: 'What the world needs now are heralds of the gospel, who are experts in humanity, familiar with their own emotions, able to share them with others, and who are, at the same time, contemplatives who have fallen in love with God.' Around this time I also began to realise that whatever we mean by 'the faith' is caught, not just taught. And I myself had to be transformed before others would be. Only to the extent that I had explored the inner complexity of my own heart would I ever be of any use to the people I served. I had to learn how to know myself well because it was myself, with my light and shadow, my sins and graces, my pretence and my authenticity, that came across in my preaching, my serving, my leadership.

And the journey continues. My life is now devoted to deepening the awareness of this sacramental vision, this spirituality of the heart, not only for the personal transformation of people's lives, but in the ministries of education, catechesis and preaching. During these final decades of my life, my ministry lies in speaking and writing on such vibrant issues.

Summer:
The Grace of Blossoming

Born to be wild

The impulse to 'launch out into the deep' is universal and insistent. But so is the fear and hesitation that so often prevents us from responding to the call in the way Christ intended.

I reached one of the 'big O's on my recent birthday. For some reason there was a striking similarity in the themes of the cards I received. Most of them were urging me into a new phase of rather desperate self-expression and risky escapades. There were pictures of breathtaking bungee jumping, parachuting out of airplanes, and death-defying goats leaping perilously across yawning chasms. I unwrapped a T-shirt recalling Jack Kerouac's 1950s novel *On the Road* in bright red and green letters.

But most of all there were motorbikes storming across endless countrysides and deserts. Some of these gleaming machines were ridden by the youthful and hairy Dennis Hopper and Peter Fonda of *Easy Rider* fame. One cutout card had a PRESS button on it that released the throttled power of an engine changing gears as it roared into the distance.

Last Easter the Harley-Davidson annual gathering took place in Killarney near where I was born. Instead of avoiding the noisy, crowded town on that weekend as many had supposed, the local people thronged the streets to see and touch the silver, purring monsters. Parents, grandparents and small children, excitedly or wistfully, were visibly stirred by these gleaming machines.

I wondered about the source of our innate desire for adventure, for new vistas, for encountering the unknown, for living at the limits. Is there a force within us that needs to be always reaching for what is beyond us, to be forever compelled to explore? Were all those cards and images but another way of expressing the restless pilgrimage of our graced nature? Were the leaping goats, the opening parachutes, the dream adventurers on the fabled Route 66 to California – were they all symbols of a God who continually beckons us, from within, to new horizons? Is there a compulsion to be free in all of us?

With the coming of summer my mother, even in her nineties, would recall for us a memory of pure delight from her early teenage years. On the rare occasions when she and my Auntie

Nell were released from the drudgery of their work, they would wheel out, not a Harley-Davidson but a rusty, ramshackle old bike. One pedalled, the other hung on for dear life as they bumped their way down a North Cork farm road – or *bohereen*, as they would have called it – both shouting at the top of their voices, 'Be gone, dull care. I give you to the winds.'

During these weeks between Easter and Pentecost we may ask whether the breaking out of the tomb is another image of all our innate longing for freedom? Can the Risen Christ be seen as a figure of humanity's relentless desire to transcend mortality? Is the Ascension an endorsement of God's irrepressible energy placed from the beginning in every human heart? Does Pentecost celebrate the imperative to 'go forth', to travel the world with open hearts and minds of light?

The compulsion towards 'beyondness', the quest towards liberation, was in Jesus' blood. He was constantly engaged in liberating people from all kinds of restrictions on their freedom, from the things that kept them constricted, from the chains that prevented their flight into another way of being. His utter reck-lessness in walking into the traps of his enemies, into the garden of his blood, up the hill of his death and into the awful tomb of his darkness and of human sin – all prepared him for the cosmic journey, the final breakthrough, that alerts and draws all of us to the margins of our own awesome possibilities.

Easter, Ascension and Pentecost inspire, gather and celebrate all the daily breakthroughs in our lives – the brave, prophetic word, the refusal to become a victim, the surrender of ego-con-trol, the telling of the truth, the courage to be. Maybe these blessed moments, in terms of heart and soul, are unknowingly symbolised in the beckoning images of those birthday cards. When you are committed to this way of living your life you have, as Janet Kalven wrote, 'set sail on another ocean without star or compass, going where the argument leads, shattering the certainties of centuries.' This is a Pentecost invitation we would often rather ignore.

There was a wildness in Jesus, as there was in John the Baptist before him: a relentless courage that was of the essence of his divine humanity. He was for ever testing the boundaries, pushing the limits of his own potential, weighing up the wishes of his Father. He was driven to take to the Jerusalem road, to confront the people who wanted to destroy him – but only so that soon he would transcend all limitations and, in doing so, empower us with the divine potential to walk the path of our own destiny.

However, while Jesus achieved the final breakthrough once for all, we are still only on the way. The journey ahead is littered with choices – to keep taking the risks of change, to keep climbing the mountain of grace, to keep leaving what is not nourishing us. On days when we are not afraid, we follow our bliss; we take the high road; we are, as Goethe said in 'The Holy Longing', 'insane for the light'. But too often the price is too high. The French novelist André Gide wrote, 'One does not discover new lands without consenting to lose sight of the shore for a very long time.' Most of us are not famous for this kind of 'launching out into the deep' – urged on the whole church by John Paul II.

Even though redeemed, we do not always choose the light. We are transplanted but we refuse to grow. A vista is revealed, but we are afraid to contemplate it. We shrink from the shadow of the Cross that falls over everything. Open horizons have been painfully won for us yet we prefer instead the safety of the circled wagons, the three secure tents of Mount Tabor. Though forgiven we do not forgive; resentment stays curled up like a snake in the fallen leaves of our lives until suddenly it strikes, and we tumble, once more, down the ladder of our good intentions.

Yet a free and beckoning God will not leave us alone – a God whose Celtic image was the Wild Goose, a God who stirs in us a passion for another country where everything is different, who urgently urges us to chase the wild dream. To travel, to search, to hope – the Pentecost imperative whispers relentlessly within us. 'In the computer metaphor of today we are hard-wired to hope,' writes Christopher Howse. 'To persevere is in our nature.' The first journey, then, in the end, is the journey inwards – into the land of our own ambiguous, infinite mystery.

To be truly human is to be for ever pursuing a subtle and elusive dream. Many grow old with the glint of adventure still in their eyes. The girl in W. B. Yeats' poem may be your lost treasure. She may be your dream companion, your dream accomplishment, your dream horizon. She may be the spirit of your never-ending Ithaca-journey, that wild, unfathomable sanctuary deep within your own heart:

> When I am old with wandering through
> hollow lands and hilly lands,
> I will find out where she has gone, and kiss
> her lips and take her hands;
> And walk among long dappled grass, and
> pluck till time and times are done,
> The silver apples of the moon, the golden
> apples of the sun.

Windows of wonder

Contemplation is not a technique to be mastered but a journey inside ourselves to become one with what already is. When we do this and glimpse what is there, it takes our breath away.

A few weeks ago I was listening to the bells of Ampleforth Abbey pealing grace across the moors and valleys of North Yorkshire. The invitation to share a week with the monks was a great honour. And a great grace. The discipline and regularity of monastic life protects the sacred setting for exploring the shy secrets of God. Together we wondered at the meaning of Incarnation – did God really become human, totally our flesh, utterly our senses, breath of our breath, heart of our heart?

As if for the first time, what began to occupy our minds then was the extent to which God is really around us, within us. Whatever our experiences of human intimacy may be, God is more intimate still. However deeply we may succeed in accessing levels of our own consciousness, God will always be deeper still. Incarnation is experienced in terms of profound earthly presence and promise. And when we glimpse and feel its meaning in the flesh, it takes our breath away.

At the 400th anniversary of Downside Abbey in 2006, Cardinal Cormac Murphy-O'Connor reminded his listeners that a monastery is not a flight from the fragility of human nature but a way of meeting it, of exploring and transforming it, of celebrating it. Our traditional mystics have written so revealingly about the holiness of the ground we walk on: it is sacred space, the eternity within every moment of the day; it is sacred time, the Holy Spirit inspiring our very breathing; it is sacred breath, the divine energy in our beating pulse; it is our sacred heart, all that is perceived through the senses – they are thresholds of the soul.

As I walked one windy evening through the rugby fields of the monastery's school, Ampleforth College, I continued wondering about the closeness of God to us, about the utter miracle of it all. Can it be true that divine peace is really and instantly available at every second, and in every place, with every experience of our senses, as accessible as our next breath and heartbeat? Does God's warming presence truly fill our most profound depths with every experience of every sense? Is it, in fact, whether we know it or not, quite impossible to avoid being centred in the very pulse-beat of heaven?

It is all too extraordinary to believe, I felt. Understandably we flinch before the realisation that we can actually experience the vibrancy of God. Surely it cannot really be as ordinary as that, we argue. The 'Other' can never be so familiarly present. That is altogether too shocking, certainly too uncomfortable. It is much easier to build a religion and keep God within it. We can live our lives then without touching the sacred at every hand's turn. That is why we are happy to regard contemplative living as the 'religious' way of getting close to God – a summit that only monks can reach.

One morning the mystic, monk and poet Thomas Merton realised, to his surprise, that contemplation is not about the acquisition of a consciousness emptied of everything except thoughts of God. It was the opposite – not a movement towards a distant God but a sinking into a deeper awareness of one's own life and to find God already there. Contemplation, he surmised, was not a different state to our usual way of being. There is only one reality. Our hours and our days are divided not between time spent with God or with the world but between those occasions when we are more, or less, aware of God's presence in our experiences – when we are more, or less, distracted from that presence by the heartaches of our work.

'It is enough to be in an ordinary human mode, with one's hunger and sleep, one's cold and warmth, rising and going to bed, putting on blankets and then taking them off, making coffee and then drinking it,' he wrote. 'Also defrosting the refrigerator, reading, meditating … Contemplation is a way of being really inside our own daily experiences. We are in contemplation when we perform the routine tasks of our lives so as to perceive in them that our lives are not little, anonymous or not important any more, but that what's timeless, eternal, is in the ordinariness of things.'

Eternity is not opposed to time. It is pure presence. That is when we experience timelessness. 'Time is eternity living dangerously!' the Kerry mystic John Moriarty believed. For those of us who feel too inadequate, too sinful to believe that any true intimacy with a Lover-God is ever even remotely possible, these are words of hope. Contemplation is not a technique to be mastered, a discipline to be perfected. It is the journey of the spirit into what is already within.

Only a few days ago a friend sent me a Masai prayer: 'May you see what you see through different eyes, hear what you hear with different ears. May you taste what you have never tasted before, and go further than yourself.' The story of God's inner being is written everywhere, strewn around us like pearls in a parking lot, like love letters in a tip, like treasure hidden in every field. All we ask for is the grace to notice and believe in this extravagance, to identify the grace place. This is the work of contemplation.

'Too often we are not present to the beauty, love and grace that brims within the ordinary moments of our lives,' Ronald Rolheiser writes. 'Our lives come laden with riches, but we are not sufficiently present to what is there.' That presence is the gift and revelation of Incarnation; it is the sheer fulfilment of it, the authenticity and truth of it. It is the miracle of mindfulness.

That is why, the holy ones tell us, the contemplative way is not really a way at all. The secret is that there is no secret. Our underlying desire is, in fact, to have no desire, apart from the desire simply to be. The place we're going to is nowhere. The task is to occupy the place we are in, but in a new and transformed way. All we have to do is simply to be present to the music of what happens, to be attentive to the mountain behind the mountain. Contemplation is something we become, not something we do. It is a way of presence, of seeing, of always being amazed.

As I was leaving Ampleforth the winds had calmed down, the air was sweet. I was still tender with mystery. Fr Paul, rather shyly, slipped one of his poems into my hand. And then, yet another window of wonder was opened for me – a deeper sense that contemplation is a dynamic, two-way encounter.

Maybe God needs to gaze at us, too, so as to wonder again and again at the incarnate shape of love's divine face:

God wants us to sit for him
not that he may paint our portrait
but that he may paint his own –
within us.

Power of the real presence

It happened to the apostles at Pentecost. It can also happen to each and every one of us, but not through church mandate or spiritual exegesis. It is the inner authority we gain when through daily, often painful, honesty we recognise our own true soul and our own essence.

Dusk was falling as we sprinkled holy water on the brown coffin in the dark grave. It was a very long day, the day of my mother's funeral. I was at the end of my strength – everything bottled up since morning. I felt a hand on my back. My friend had arrived. The healing tears began to flow. It was the touch that did it.

We notice those who are graced with a profound presence – it is in the way some teachers teach, some check-out assistants wait for you, some priests say Mass. We notice it from time to time when parents listen and talk to their children, when someone takes control in a crisis. We feel safe, and known, by such people. The blind holy man could tell the state of soul of his visitors by the sound of their approaching footsteps. It is hard to stay closed in the aura of sensitive presence. The poet e.e. cummings wrote:

... you open always petal by petal myself as Spring opens
(touching skilfully, mysteriously) her first rose ...
... nobody, not even the rain has such small hands.

People with presence ground grace. It is what human beings are created to do. Nor should this be a surprising revelation for Christians. Christianity is the protector and champion of humanity's greatest boast – its unique claim to be designed and inhabited by God. It was in the human form that God chose to reveal the real presence of salvation. And Jesus explained to St Teresa how our redeemed senses hold and carry the divine compassion that saves the world.

So when, for instance, we live in our true presence, then we look, without filters, at people, and the grace in our eyes carries a mysterious love straight to their hearts. When we speak with people from our blessed essence, our words of pure truth open for them casements on to fields of hope. We listen to them in the stillness of our being, and the fierceness of our faith begins to vibrate in their bodies too. We touch them, and in the integrity of our surrendered selves, our hands become, for them, the hands of Christ. Our best spiritual directors and writers know this well.

We believe that this is so because it was in the physical earthiness of the utterly human Jesus that the truest way of God's closeness to Creation, to each person, began. 'In the beginning was the Presence.'

There was an attractiveness about the reality of Jesus' company, about the way he looked and listened to people, that they simply fell in love with. So utterly present was he to himself, and to his heavenly father, that his very physical being was suffused with vibrant energy. It leaped out, without his bidding, when he was touched by another. It was the tangible presence of the wounded Risen Christ that unblocked the troubled heart of Thomas.

To be solidly grounded in, centred on, and shining with divine power is the way we are meant to be. Thomas Merton wrote: 'We all exist solely for this – to be the human place God has chosen for his presence, his manifestation, his epiphany.' Given that this is so, our senses are truly thresholds of the soul, sensory sacramentals of healing presence. In our truest humanity, we are walking sacraments of the Being from whom we've come, but to whom we are always returning, too ...

It is an exciting rediscovery of our essential identity. 'My deepest me is God,' repeated St Catherine of Genoa. 'We are God's words,' Merton wrote. 'We echo him, we signify and contain him.' This is to be utterly ourselves. 'Awaken to the mystery of being here, and enter the quiet immensity of your own presence,' wrote John O'Donohue. 'May all that is unforgiven in you be released. May all that is unlived in you blossom into a future graced with love.' And when we are utterly ourselves we are utterly divine.

There is a raw and wretched kind of purification that we have to suffer if we are ever to live, move and have our being within this incarnate integrity. The inauthentic self, with its ego-masks, is a false presence. We must recognise first, after daily, painful, inner honesty, the shape of our own naked soul. We are continually deceived by the insubstantial mirage that confused our First Parents. But every time we eat the bread at the table of truth, when God's own essence intimately informs and transforms our ever-drifting selves, that real presence is again re-aligned and consecrated.

Maybe only children and saints want to be nobody else. To enter that grounded place of transparency, where our every breath is a true inspiration, where every word is an Incarnate one, where presence itself becomes an unbidden absolution, we must, like Jesus did, die many deaths. We must substitute a personal Calvary for institutional conformity. It is how souls are saved. This I found to be equally true in recent visitations with the still and silent monks on Caldey Island and with the urgent, active missionaries in Ecuador.

Real presence and inner authority go together. Inner authority is the outcome of a graced and grounded experience of a fleshed God. It comes from a desire to be nothing but the dwelling place of our tremendous lover. That is the essential me. To be nobody else. In recent times our spiritual storytellers remind us that we will never overhear a kingfisher saying it wants to be an eagle, a daisy wanting to be a rose, an ant wanting to be a lizard. Only the humanoid wants to be someone else.

Everything in nature is utterly present. That is why its praise is perfect. 'Stop shouting at me,' St Francis said to the rose. Because Francis was being true to his naked nature, and the rose to hers, they were both lighting the place up. The rose, Richard Rohr explains, does not need to prove itself, or convert you to its side. It knows full well that it is a rose. Its inner authority is complete. If our inner authority were complete too, even if silent, the world would say to us also: 'I hear you. Stop shouting.' That is the power of real presence. It happened to the apostles at Pentecost.

When the world meets people whose centre of gravity is within their authentic selves, it draws close to them like moths to a flame, like metal to a magnet. The inner authority we need must be straight from the Trinity that is the soul of our solid flesh. It can no longer come from church mandate alone, or scriptural exegesis. Only those with inner authority have the soul-force and presence to transform violence and fear, to restore peace. They alone create vital new space for transforming presence. The rest of us re-arrange the furniture in the Upper Room.

Mystery in a drop of wine

A moment at Charing Cross Tube station brings a brief revelation that, unlike between the train and the platform, there is no gap between the innate God of our hearts and the God of Jesus.

Do you have a favourite place, a place that stirs your heart, that holds great memories for one reason or another? At the risk of placedropping, I can think of Cape Breton in Nova Scotia, Taranaki in New Zealand, Sydney Harbour Bridge, Iona, Robbin Island off Cape Town. However, the one I select is, of all places, London's Charing Cross station. For me it has become like a small Underground sacrament.

The last time I passed through it, on the Bakerloo Line, was just after Easter Sunday when the imagination is sensitised to the nearness of mystery. I have always associated the place with Francis Thompson's poem 'The Kingdom of God', picturing angels ascending and descending between heaven and Platform 3. Synchronically, almost scarily, this is what happened to me as the train drew into the station. While only half aware of the sea of different faces and garments, and half-listening to the lilt and timbre of many accents, I began to perceive in a more focused way the colours and textures, shapes and sounds flowing from the human panoply around me.

In the sudden spring warmth they seemed to shimmer with divinity. It was one of those moments of disclosure that many people experience a few times in their lives, when, caught off guard, time stands still, and a deeper awareness breaks through. It was a gift of grace, when God's presence seemed to be pressing in on me more intensely than usual. It was all so mysterious, yet so intimate and energising. I still remember my delight at the realisation that the power within Creation, the author of all the beauty I was just then experiencing, was, in fact, personally involved with me, utterly satisfying and fulfilling. There was also a strong sense of the part I played in this whole panorama. A line from de Chardin came to me: 'What I call my body is not part of the universe which I possess totally; it is the whole universe which I possess partly.'

Even though my experience was profound, it did not last long – just for the brief space between the opening and closing of those sliding doors at Charing Cross station. In one sense this unsolicited epiphany changed nothing; in another sense it changed everything. It certainly left me with many disturbing questions.

I struggle now, for instance, to find the lovely face of this deeply felt gracious presence, in the content and doctrines of any rigorous religion. The alluring, compelling excitement of the warm heart of Being itself does not always find its home in the house of institutional religion. The divine features in the pulsing centre of a living universe are often scarcely recognisable in a more parsimonious, ecclesiastical deity. The image of God offered by many churches struggles to resonate with the vibrant, intoxicating God of Creation, of Jesus and of human hearts. Thomas Aquinas said that a mistake in our understanding of Creation will necessarily cause a mistake in our understanding of God. Have too much love and beauty been lost in translation?

Einstein cherished 'a feeling of utter humility towards the unattainable secrets of the harmony of the cosmos' and saw himself, before the mystery, as he put it, 'in the position of a little child entering a huge library filled with books in many languages'. Here we have the wonder of the mystics, the silence of the contemplatives, the new images of a sacramental vision. Fearful religion, adrift from its source, blocks out God's mystical flow in and through all things. It cannot cope with a God so big.

Only in the Son of Man, the Human One, is the perfect fit found. Only in him is the vision sharp, the truth intact, the revelation accurate. The heart of God and the heart of Creation beat in tune and time in his human heart. There is a traditional Christian vision that places Jesus within the very structure of the cosmos itself: 'Christ is the firstborn of all Creation, for in him all things in heaven and on earth were created.'

Here we have the fleshed love, extravagance and wild artistry of our devoted Creator now incarnate in this uniquely graced man. There is no gap, dislocation or dissonance between the innate God of our hearts, of nature, of everything beautiful, and the God of Jesus. Jesus brings a tangible focus and a physical presence to the hunches and intuitions of the human race from the very beginning. Everything about Jesus is of a piece with the natural expectations and hopes of the whole human race, of Creation itself, and of my own Charing Cross moment. Revelation, according to Thomas Aquinas, is bound in two volumes, the volume of Creation and of Scripture.

Ronald Rolheiser believes that this concept challenges the imagination, implying far more than we normally dare think. 'The fact that Christ is cosmic and that nature is shaped in his likeness means God's face is manifest everywhere. If physical Creation is patterned on Christ, then we must search for God not just in our scriptures, in our saints and in our churches, but in the raw energy, colour and beauty of the physical, be that the beauty of a sunset or of a symphony.'

Now here is the question that is filling my mind. Christ, we know, is bigger than the historical churches, and has influences prior and beyond human history itself. But where, in our experience of church, is the God of Creation, the God of Jesus and the God of religion brought together and revealed as one and the same mystery truly at home with us here and now? Where, today, in our liturgy, do we find an imaginative focus for the uniting and celebrating of those three faces of God?

Like an oasis in a religious desert, the Eucharist is one such place. Pope Benedict, in his recent *Sacramentum Caritatis*, points out that 'God allows himself to be glimpsed first in Creation and in the beauty and harmony of the cosmos.' He then writes, 'the Christian people in giving thanks to God through the Eucharist, should be conscious that they do so in the name of all Creation … The Eucharist itself powerfully illuminates human history and the whole cosmos.'

The Eucharist protects, develops and expresses the divine magnificence and energy in all the living forms that dance on our planet. Without it we would forget 'the new story' of the universe, we would deny our sacred history, we would lose our essential connectedness with the ground of our being in the whole evolutionary process. 'The fullness of joy is to behold God in everything and everything in God,' wrote the mystic Julian of Norwich.

John Paul II, in his *Ecclesia de Eucharistia*, took delight in the cosmic character of the Eucharist. 'Yes, cosmic!' he wrote, 'Because even when the Eucharist is celebrated on the humble altar of a country church, it is always, in some way, celebrated on the altar of the world. It unites heaven and earth. It embraces and permeates all Creation.' In the Eucharist of Jesus, the fiery heart of the universe and the mighty heart of God slip down our throat in the same small drop of wine. The rest is wonder and silence.

Home before dark

Advancing age is a time of looking back over the way people have come, and sorting the essence of a lifetime on earth. But it is also a period of looking forward – to the homeland to which God calls the faithful to return.

A few days ago a neighbour called to the presbytery with news about a local 'old folks' party. Did she want me to say a few words at it? I asked. Or to borrow our hall? No, she was inviting me to attend because I was old. 'And bring your own cup and plate.' It was then I realised how deep in denial I was about my age. A recent survey published by *Help the Aged* reveals that one in five people have lied about how old they were.

There is often little grace in the way we regard our final years. We see them as the last, threatening, empty lap in the race of our lives. Our legs are tiring. The ground is rising. The applause is muted. The crowd is departing. There is a sense of loneliness, almost of abandonment. We rarely see those years as the welcome threshold of our final homecoming.

In John's gospel, Jesus speaks about one day bringing us with him to our home in heaven. There is always a strong emotional charge in the notion of 'coming home'. One day I asked my mother about the most vivid moment in her life. (I had presumed, as you do, that my birth would have been her most unforgettable experience.) It was, she said, the morning she awoke to the sight of the Kerry hills, along the southern Irish coast, when, after years of work in the US, the homecoming ship drew close to Cobh harbour in 1920. Her heart nearly burst with happiness that morning, she said, and, 75 years later, the tears of memory still welled up in her eyes. Old age is like the elephant in the living room even of the middle-aged. It is anxiously perceived as a time of loss. This most vulnerable time of our life has no real catechesis to take away the edge of fear. Part of a preparation for growing old would remind us of the eternal energy that never leaves us; a kind of energy that sleeps, neglected, within us while we are relentlessly obsessed with the driven routines that must be melted down again in retirement.

Negotiating our advancing years is like pausing on a mountain top to look back at the way we have come. There is a sense of being able to blow away the chaff of many things, so as to reveal the essential wheat of our time on earth. Now only the essence remains. Ideally, the final decades will have a purity about them, a pared-down core that shines with a recovered innocence.

Shortly before his death Michael Mayne wrote about the *cantus firmus* of his life, the enduring melody that never left him. But Michael's beautiful soul had first to be surrendered to the terrible blows of the carver's hands, before it rediscovered the eternal music of his youth. In his magnificent 'The Faces at Braga', the poet David Whyte suggests the harvest of such surrender.

Our faces would fall away
until we, growing younger toward death
every day, would gather all our flaws in celebration
to merge with them perfectly,
impossibly, wedded to our essence,
full of silence from the carver's hands.

Finding out who we really are is like a personal, lifelong Passover. Too many tapes from the past have labelled us too soon. They have tricked us into a false identity. The final phase is the time when the mirror is clearest, revealing, maybe for the first time, our authentic voice and our own name. We begin to see with the sure eyes of Jesus. We finally whisper our 'yes' to the mystery and miracle of who we really are, and always were. At the moment of death, some people's faces light up with an astonished look of recognition. They go home with shining eyes.

John O'Donohue refers to this transition through surface diminishment as a sacramental moment. The ultimate fragmentation and peeling away can reveal what was too long concealed. Old age can be compared to a time of theatre when the bare bones of advanced years are the actor's ultimate disguise. Within that old body lies pure distilled essence, the *unum necessarium*, a still untapped well now ready to let its life-giving waters flow free. Your life is a Eucharist and you are the priest that gathers, transforms and celebrates it. It is not the amount of work, or length of your days that matter; it is their consecration.

This *eukharistia* of our lives is our gratitude for them. In *A*

View from the Ridge Morris West repeats what Meister Eckhart had already suggested, that once we reach a certain age there should be only one phrase left in our vocabulary – 'thank you'. With every birthday, gratitude should deepen until it colours every aspect of our life. Ronald Rolheiser adds, however, that only forgiveness sets us free to say that word in its essential power.

All of this is the inner work of the soul at its most fruitful. It may have little to do with institutional rituals. In old age we have permission to move beyond the once-useful, now debilitating boundaries that fence in what the poet Mary Oliver calls 'our one wild and precious life'. This is the time to stand outside all that has confined and defined us over the decades – false traditions, soulless systems. Joseph Campbell asks us to look for that part of us which is no longer 'beholden', that stands outside the normal structures that have settled so heavily on us. We are made for more.

It isn't the illusory achievements and promotions that matter in the end, Henri Nouwen believed. It is the depth of our humanity, the experience of being loved. 'The time is indeed growing short for me,' he wrote, 'but that knowledge sets me free to prevent mourning from depressing me. (It) can now deepen my quiet desire for the day when I realise that the many kisses and embraces I received today were simple incarnations of the eternal embrace of the Lord himself.'

A new homeland draws into view when, as senior citizens, we start living from within. Our souls are always young. They have preserved, in a safe place, the fields of dreams that once lay beautifully across the landscapes of our childhood. It is in these fields, and in no other, where the seeds of our God-like beauty were first nurtured, that our eternal harvest will be reaped. We do not outgrow our childhood. We grow into it more fully as we grow older. And it is only in heaven that we will possess it completely.

No matter how old we are, we still have time to let the light in, to break down the barriers we once erected between us and our truest self. Nothing is so sad as regretting, on our deathbed, our unlived lives, our untold stories, our unsung songs. Yet, in God's extravagance, during those last times, everything lost –

the dream, the innocence, the melody – can all be restored. And if, one of these summer evenings, you faintly hear again your mother's voice calling you in because the night is coming, your eyes will start to shine because, as the house of heaven draws ever closer, you will recognise it, with astonishment, as the home you never left.

Painful, slow redemption

Irish churchmen and women – and politicians too – should resist attempts at quick closure to the shocking revelations of criminal mental, physical and sexual abuse perpetrated on the country's most vulnerable children. Rather, they should spend a lot of time of their knees.

It was early on the morning of 21 May that the first emails arrived. Grieving friends were writing about the saddest day for church and state in Ireland. Since then, both friends and enemies of Roman Catholicism have been listing in graphic detail the shameful catalogue of physical and emotional torment, the savage beatings and unbelievable abuse that were endemic to the clerical and political system in the church-run institutions of the twentieth century.

On that day *The Irish Times* editorial described the Ryan report – 'The Report of the Commission to Inquire into Child Abuse' – as 'the map of an Irish hell'. Unlike some previous documentation, the editorial explained, this account of systematic cruelty could not be denied, or ignored. It was the result of a system that demanded silence through fear, a methodology handed down through several generations of priests, brothers and nuns.

Most commentators pointed to that deliberate silence as the most serious failure of both church and state. This was the kind of silence that has outraged the victims of abuse. It is the unspoken collusion with darkness, they believed. It is institutional power at its worst – the prolonged, corrosive cover-up to save its own face at any cost. They spoke of a country 'burning with fury'.

These are very hard, even terrifying, words, and a first instinct is to react defensively, to emphasise the unquantifiable treasures of the church's goodness. But that is not the way to go just now. For the church today, it is the time to listen to an awful truth. The contents of the Ryan report, the depth of feeling among Catholics across the world, are almost too much to bear or to believe.

Deeply disturbed leaders of church and state are searching for the sources of this terrible inhumanity. How could such high ideals in the pursuit of spiritual perfection become so shockingly debased in a holy institution? How could those men and women, the great majority of whom entered their congregations and seminaries with a loving determination to follow the teachings of Jesus Christ, descend to such levels of behaviour?

Having acknowledged the valiant work of the church in Ireland, *The Irish Times'* religious affairs editor, Patsy McGarry, wondered whether 'a dark theology of fallen human nature with a propensity to evil allowed a climate where such viciousness could be constantly visited on children'. This may well be at the root of some shameful behaviour in our ailing church.

Studies have revealed that Catholics in the United States, who were brought up to believe in the God who punished people eternally in hell, were the most likely to vote for the Iraq war, and to support the use of torture to protect their country. How did we ever expect to erase in later life the indelible traces cut into small souls by those visions of unending torture at the hands of a judging deity? Such a poisoned cradling was bound to produce a damaged harvest.

Albert Einstein reminded us of two pertinent truths for today. One is that 'the surface is the last thing to collapse'. Everything can seem to be going well; we're holding it all together during a bad patch; God will see us through. Then one day the very surface collapses because its hidden support turns out to be rotten. The publication of the Ryan report marks the collapse of a religious surface in Irish life.

The other truth Einstein held was that 'the mindset that causes its own inner collapse can never carry the seeds of its own renewal'. The necessary paradigm shift we long for cannot happen only from within any more. A new source, maybe from a place as yet unknown to us, must be found for another start, a new healing, a new hope. Otherwise, in systemic thinking, left to itself, the organisation will clone itself back into business as usual.

That is why many fear that religious and state leaders are now pushing too fast for closure without learning any vital lessons. What alarms them now is that in the wake of the recent report, church leaders are already looking anxiously for a premature closure. The experience of an abuse, they say, that has turned you into a depressive, unemotional father, a hopeless alcoholic, a suicidal introvert, just cannot be set aside like that. Regaining a lost trust takes ages. Too many take the pain to the grave.

Whatever the outcome, the church needs to spend a lot of time on her knees now, preparing for some kind of death out of which it can be born again, reclaiming the innocence and the powerlessness of its servant-leader. The fault line runs deeply through its length and breadth. It runs so deeply that often it can scarcely be perceived from within. That is why its redemption will be both painful and slow.

Wherever and whenever it is called for, the church needs to replace a heart of stone with a compassionate one, an arrogant heart with a humble one. When a community becomes an organisation, when law rather than spirit rules, when the mystical vision is lost to the moralising mentality, then dreadful things can happen. Dominative control replaces the ministering presence of Jesus; authoritarianism replaces a personal inner authority. Clericalism is about power; priesthood is about service. But it is the prophetic that is needed now.

We need charismatic leaders as well as functional ones, transparent leaders rather than organisation men. Otherwise self-preservation and scapegoating become all-important. This is evident when the church forgets to first weep with the broken victims before explaining and defending itself. It all depends where one's treasure is!

There is a necessary waiting time – to feel the shame of the abused, to hear in our soul the abandoned lament of theirs, to stay in that place of utter confusion and desolation – and even then, we will never even remotely glimpse the awful anguish they will carry to the grave.

As we celebrate this 'Year of Paul' we remember one of his finest attributes – his courage. Courage for God's broken little ones to learn again to hope, for the church to face its sins, for the guilty ones to search into their own hearts, and for all of us to acknowledge the part we are playing, by our silence, in the whole sorry story. Paul could not keep silent when truth was compromised. For him, as for Jesus, his power lay in his utter transparency.

Reconciliation has little meaning while anger rages. For how can repeatedly abused people ever forgive the church? How does a humiliated, human/divine institution forgive itself? Can people trust the church any more to critique itself deeply and rediscover the authentic meaning of the reign of God? What processes can be set up to begin the slow path to courageous conversations? And how do we all make sure that we are trying to work together in the spirit of a real love of truth?

'I have never heard my name,' a victim told the abuse commission. Is this when angels weep? May that terrible cry to heaven never be heard again from any of God's children, especially from those placed in our care in homes, schools and parishes. 'Oh do not grieve, my beautiful and beloved child. My heart breaks with love for you. You are breath of my breath and pulse of my pulse. Even though no one has told you, or called you by name, listen closely to your own small heart.'

Nothing is ever completely hopeless. If we doubt that then indeed all is lost. Sooner or later, grace will always find a way to enter in. And in that, at least, we can trust.

Lost but for words

Jesus was not only the Son of God, he was the Word of God made flesh. And in using words to express our love for others, we reflect his love for us.

> We met under a shower of bird-notes.
> Fifty years passed, love's moment
> In a world in servitude to time.
> She was young; I kissed with my eyes closed
> And opened them on her wrinkles.
> *(From 'A Marriage', by R. S. Thomas)*

Tucked away in some part of our soul there will be a precious memory of a season of love. It may have been in our childhood, our teenage years or last August, but one moment will always be special. Even if our love will pass away, as R. S. Thomas puts it, with 'one sigh no heavier than a feather' the memory will stay fresh, etched into our hearts for ever. At such times the language of love comes naturally to us.

Without this language, received or given, the silence cries out. After Mass at Newcastle Cathedral last month a young man waited for a word with me. In his hand he held a copy of a book I had signed for him a few years earlier at the request of a friend. 'With lots of love,' I had written. 'I just want to thank you,' he said earnestly. 'No one ever wrote or said those words to me. It was making me ill.' And I hadn't even known him. How fearful and slow we are to talk lovingly.

And yet our best words of love have all the power of God to reveal the unique and divine truth in each one. When a lover says to the beloved, 'You are beautiful', the grateful reply, 'You have made me so', is often made. To be sure, there is a sense in which this is true. But it is not the whole truth. What happens, I think, is that we draw out and reveal the beauty already there within another. We create the circumstances for the shy and frightened loveliness in the other to emerge. We then become catalysts of transcendence. When we are awake to our own beauty, we open the eyes of the sleeping beauty in another. This is the most sacred, sacramental moment. Our truest, total presence to all that is around us is the language of love.

A kind of dance goes on in the language of love. Whether

with words or gestures we are weaving what Mícheál Ó Siadhail calls 'a fragile city'. Love is a flow, a giving and a receiving. 'To keep the right balance between closeness and distance,' wrote Henri Nouwen, 'requires hard work, especially since the needs of each person may be quite different at a given time. One might want to be held while the other looks for independence. A perfect balance seldom occurs, but the honest and open search for that balance can give birth to a beautiful dance worthy to behold.'

All our teaching will be sterile until it springs from a full heart. Three times Jesus so tenderly drew out the fullness of Peter's thrice-denied love before entrusting to him the immense work of nourishing God's people. Only when Peter had his love for his great friend restored did Jesus feel that he was ready to teach. Mark Van Doren wrote a poem about the teacher he remembered most:

> It must unfold as grace, inevitably, necessarily,
> as tomcats stretch: in such a way he lolled upon his desk
> and fell in love again before our very eyes
> again, again – how many times again! –
> with Dante, Chaucer, Shakespeare, Milton's Satan,
> as if his shameless, glad, compelling love
> were all he really wanted us to learn …

It is only when the language of knowledge and the language of love come together that lives are transformed. Loving, in fact, comes before knowing, not after it. You cannot really know something if you do not first love it. 'Only the heart knows in the full sense of the word,' Karl Rahner writes. 'Really interior knowledge, knowledge that grasps something completely and is more than a list of facts, is knowledge of the heart, the human centre, which knows by experience and by suffering – the human centre where spirit and body, light and love dwell undivided in one chasm. In the final analysis, knowledge is but the radiance of love.'

Sadly, the language of doctrine and liturgy is not always the language of love. Too often it is used for other purposes. A personal relationship with Jesus is often lost in the pursuit of ordered participation by the worshipping assembly. Without the experience of a personal love of Jesus, scripture scholar Raymond Brown warns us, church membership can miss the central meaning of the Incarnation – an intimate gazing at the face of our Saviour.

We may be experts in exegesis, theology and homiletics, yet lack the loving power and inner authority that moves people, because our own souls are not personally and passionately engaged. Our words and rubrics as welcomer, reader, minister of Communion, celebrant, though perfectly rehearsed, will not be the language of love. People's hearts are not touched. The second half of John's gospel is an intimate poem of an extraordinary love. For John, this intimacy is the point of everything else. Without the tender laying of his head on the breast of Jesus, for John, God's whole plot is lost.

There is a reluctance in us to believe this. We prefer a safer, dutiful kind of relationship. Many are uncomfortable when God is addressed with the words and images of close friends, of lovers, and of mothers and their children. Ronald Rolheiser refers to the loss, in our churches, of the loving sounds and coaxing words, along with the gentle cadence that we first heard from our mothers when they lured us into self-awareness. What is needed in theology, spirituality and catechesis, he holds, are 'caressing, gentle, beckoning voices that teach us how to hear and speak the language of love,' leading us out of the darkness of our fear, awakening us to a recognition of the face of God, our mother.

Jesus actually was, and is, in his utter humanity, the mother-tongue of God. The gospels speak of Christ as 'the Word' – the Word of Love. Like this Word, then, all words – especially those of hierarchy, of liturgy, of teaching and preaching – are small incarnations of Being that is Love. In 'Words for It' Julia Cameron captures the yearnings of both mother and lover for bringing words to life:

> I wish I could take language and fold it like cool, moist rags.
> I would lay words on your forehead. I would
> wrap words on your wrist.
> 'There, there,' my words would say – or
> something even better.

I would ask them to murmur, 'Hush' and "Shh,
shh, it's all right.'
I would ask them to hold you all night.
I wish I could take language and daub and
soothe and cool
Where fever blisters and burns, where fever
turns yourself against you.
I wish I could take language and heal the words
that were the wounds
You have no name for.

Summer is the season of dreams

Many of us have felt the pull of something deep down inside ourselves, and also outside of us, that we long for almost without knowing it, and that the world only lets us glimpse before it vanishes below the horizon.

With the warmth of the sun, and the long evenings, the poets in us, the artists within, find their voice again. Summer is a time when we become more conscious of our mystery and its destiny.

Summer loosens the edges of our control. It awakens the deep and buried dreams that sleep in winter. There is a kind of ache for something that is always beyond, a restlessness that never goes away.

It is easy to stir that wistful desire. The first swallow can do it, or the smell of rain on the ground after a hot day, or the ring of church bells carried over the meadows, or down our streets, by the breezes of a summer evening.

Because our human condition is never complete, there is almost always within us a yearning for wholeness. We carry intimations of a finer destiny. We intuitively search for a lost paradise. We have blurred memories of a field of dreams on which we once played, we hear vague whispers of something yet to come, something for which we feel we were made in the first place.

Is there a subtle compulsion to transcendence in every heart? Is there an intuition of another existence somewhere in the soul of the millions who drive, walk, cycle to work each morning? Does the mother of a young family look out of the window of her comfortable home and sometimes dream of a brighter place? And to whom could she dare reveal her secret loneliness?

Does the successful businessman, at the height of his career, watch the morning fields fly by from his first-class seat, and wonder if that's all there is? In the evenings of summer do we all experience something like that – the nurse, the teacher, the check-out assistant? When enjoying the warm sun and a glass of wine does the traveller long for another horizon, the rebel for another cause, the priest for another god?

Intimations of a deeper joy in another homeland come only in scattered and subtle glimpses. In *The Wind in the Willows* Kenneth Grahame describes Ratty and Mole's meeting with the

Piper at the Gates of Dawn. 'It's gone,' sighed the Rat, sinking back in his seat again. 'So beautiful and strange and new! Since it was to end so soon, I almost wish I had never heard it. For it has roused a longing in me that is pain, and nothing seems worth while but just to hear that sound once more and go on listening to it for ever. No! There it is again!' he cried, alert once more. Entranced, he was silent for a long space, spellbound. 'Now it passes on and I begin to lose it,' he said presently. 'O Mole! The beauty of it ...'

We are congenitally overcharged for this earth. We are infinite spirits in finite conditions. We carry a helpless attraction for the beauty that gave us birth. We are *capax mundi, capax Dei* (knowing Creation, knowing God) but trapped in the limit-conditions of time and space. Is it any wonder then that we have silent struggles with our existential emptiness and insatiability?

In 'The Buried Life' Matthew Arnold wrote:

> But often, in the world's most crowded streets,
> But often, in the din of strife
> There rises an unspeakable desire
> After the knowledge of our buried life:
> ... A longing to inquire
> Into the mystery of this heart which beats
> So wild, so deep in us – to know
> Whence our lives come and where they go.

There is an undertow of unfulfilment that only union with our source and our destiny will heal and complete. To be tormented by restlessness is one of the many frustrating consequences of being both human and divine at the same time! There is no escape from the echoes of an infinite horizon. We live in the thin place where mysteries meet.

Even Jesus did not escape this innate desire for something more. 'I came to bring fire to the earth, and how I wish it were already kindled.' (Luke 12:49) It was, in fact, because of the fleshing of the Word in the humanity of Jesus, that we Christians can make some sense of the ceaseless, human longing arising from our innate coding for possessing eternity.

In *The Holy Longing* Goethe writes of how God's excessive love for the world is mirrored and echoed in our own human hearts. At its root, all longing is a longing for home, all life a de-sire to return to the love from which we have come. Do we ac-cept the unavoidable truth that nothing except total union with the essence of life itself, an ultimate intimacy with the love that fires all living things, will ever bring the peace we spend our days searching for? That is the distant but unrelenting voice that keeps calling to us like a far wave.

The theologian Karl Rahner was well aware of the pathos of this apparently hopeless, sometimes unbearable, orientation of our human nature. 'In the torment of the insufficiency of every-thing attainable', he wrote, 'we come to understand, that here in this life all symphonies remain unfinished.' The dream, the music continue in heaven. But without the pain. Even though our tender imagination may be crushed in us as children by careless caretakers, the guardian angel of our desire will never abandon us to a dreamless place. In 'The Thread', Denise Levertov wrote:

> Something is very gently,
> invisibly, silently
> pulling at me – a thread
> or net of threads
> finer than cobweb and as
> elastic … Not fear
> but a stirring of wonder makes me
> catch my breath when I feel
> the tug of it when I thought
> it had loosened itself and gone.

Autumn
The Grace of Fading

The most difficult leap

It is said that only by completely trusting at least one person can you be deemed psychologically healthy. Similarly it is only through having complete faith in Christ, complete trust, rather than slavishly following the rules, that we will be saved.

Between sessions, one warm afternoon, I walked down from the Retreat House to the pier. At the same time a family arrived there for a swim. Two teenagers quickly dived in. The water rippled a metre or so below the edge of the pier.

The mother looked on while a younger member of the family made several unsuccessful efforts to follow his siblings in. They were calling him to join them but he was afraid to jump. Again and again, his face tight with determination, he would run up to the edge, only to grind to a halt in frustration. My heart twisted because a small boy was still trying fearfully to leap inside me too.

It was time for Mass so I had to start back. As I climbed the winding road that curved away from the pier below, I heard a sudden shout of joy. I turned in time to see the bright splash. Tears pricked my eyes as I quietly applauded the moment. It was only a daily occurrence, but for me, just then, it was more. In our common humanity I had shared something with the boy, and I felt a ripple of absolution for the numberless failures to trust the waters of my own life.

Few find trusting easy. There is, as Dostoevsky wrote, 'a temporary surrender of security' every time we trust and risk any kind of positive change. Taking a new step, uttering a new word, moving beyond familiar thought patterns and mindsets, is what people fear most. The unknown is seen as the enemy. That is why to trust is to have courage. 'Courage', Paul Tillich said, 'is the trusting affirmation of one's own being in spite of the powers of non-being.'

For many betrayed people the possibility of trusting again is a bridge too far. To be deceived, to have been betrayed, burns a hole in the soul. It takes a lot of holding and healing to regain the courage to trust. At some painful level most of us know this only too well. And we often carry these unhealed memories to the grave. For this we pay too high a price. 'Why is it that some people do not bear fruit?' asked Meister Eckhart. 'Because they cannot trust either God or themselves. Love cannot distrust.' Challenging words. Yet a moment's reflection will show us that without some element of trust it is as impossible to grow and 'bear fruit', even to survive at all, as it is to live without breathing.

The ability to trust depends to a very great extent on our childhood experiences. All through childhood there is a constant struggle between the forces of trust and mistrust in the daily encounters of the child: are my parents trustworthy? Is the world trustworthy? Am I trustworthy? 'One is able to trust,' Andrew Greeley writes, 'because one is confident in oneself, and because of such confidence he can take the risk of conceding complete freedom to the other; if the other rejects me, then I am still me and worthwhile. Alas, such confidence is not easy to come by, and God protect the poor person whose first attempts at self-disclosure are harshly rejected.'

In *The Transparent Self*, Sidney M. Jourard offers a definition of a psychologically healthy person as one 'who displays the ability to make himself fully known to at least one other significant human being'. For most people, perhaps surprisingly, this is an almost impossible challenge. There is such a strong tendency to hide from intimacy, to fear exposure. Deep is the ache to be known and loved, but deeper is the fear and pain of rejection. No wonder John Powell's *Why Am I Afraid to Tell You Who I Am?* became a perennial bestseller.

God reached an amazing level of trust in becoming a frail baby, thus placing the future of the world in human hands. 'What God does first and best and most is to trust people with their moment in history,' writes Matthew Fox. 'He trusts them to do what must be done for the sake of the whole community.' God was prepared to take the gamble. There is no safe way to trust. Control must be lost. Trusting makes us very vulnerable. We become easy targets.

Psychotherapists and psychologists such as Rollo May and Abraham Maslow have no doubt about the necessity of trust in our lives – and about the resistance we offer to the very life-quality that sets us free to grow. We resist because we grow tired of crying. We want to avoid further pain. And yet, after grace, whenever we try to see everything – ourselves and the world – against the infinite horizon of incarnate compassion and power, we are drawn again to trust it. We begin to see the present and the future as a safe and loving mother who yearns for our trust, longing for us to abandon ourselves to her care. It is not surprising, I suppose, that I receive so many requests 'to write something on trust'. We know to our cost that trust is a casualty of contemporary, sophisticated life. Much of this erosion of trust in political life centres on high-level scandals and the Iraq war. In big business, human greed has led to an unprecedented exploitation of the powerless and the poor, with the consequent collapse of trust in the system. In the church itself, more than ever before, accelerated by the paedophile phenomenon, there is a double crisis of trust developing – between people and their priests, and between priests and their bishops.

A recent Sunday Gospel (eleventh in Ordinary Time) told the story of Jesus' visit to the house of Simon the Pharisee. It was there that he allowed the woman 'with the bad name in the town' to wash and dry his feet with her tears and her hair. Unlike the encounter with Simon, between the woman and Jesus there was an exquisite, intimate kind of confidence and trust. Confronted with such a moment, most of us would have withdrawn in confusion, but Jesus honoured the unknown woman, seeing her as beautiful friend rather than as threatening stranger.

In the end, it is not in our perfect observance of religious practice that we are set free from our insecurities, but by trusting the human heart of a person. The second reading of the same Sunday reminds us that 'trust in Christ rather than fidelity to the Law is what saves us'. There comes a time for most of us when only this blind faith in incarnate love will see us through.

Perhaps it was during such a harrowing hour that Cardinal Newman wrote: 'Whatever, wherever I am, I can never be thrown away. If I am in sickness, my sickness may serve him; in perplexity, my perplexity may serve him. He does nothing in vain. He knows what he is about. He may take away my friends. He may throw me among strangers. He may make me feel desolate, make my spirits sink, hide my future from me – still he knows what he is about. Therefore I will trust him.'

Now and for ever more

The special graces that permeate childhood may appear lost to adults, but it is possible to believe that children glimpse a foretaste of the joys of heaven.

Late summer evenings can make our childhood memories silently ambush us and carry us away to secret places. There are strange and subtle stirrings in the heart – sudden, unbidden glimpses, pressing invitations to revisit, for a fleeting moment, our past losses and joys.

My mother warned me, even as a boy, about the later memories that would bless and burn within me. She spoke wistfully about the ways we mourn our unfulfilled dreams. How achingly right she was. Dylan Thomas in his 'Poem in October' was no stranger to such grief:

> And I saw in the turning so clearly a child's
> Forgotten mornings when he walked with his mother
> Through the parables of sunlight
> And the legends of the green chapels
> And the twice told fields of infancy
> That his tears burned my cheeks and his heart
> moved in mine.

It is difficult to write dispassionately about childhood. It is too sacred, too much intimately a part of us. There is a haunting kind of poignancy running through our memories, a touching pathos, the struggle to express something inexpressible and very beautiful. There is also a constant desire to return to that primal state as though everything afterwards was somehow a disappointment.

Poets strive to capture those memories of childhood that carry shades of the numinous, of a familiarity with the divine, and then, of a gradual loss, in time, of that graced intimation. William Wordsworth believed that we are born 'trailing clouds of glory' and that 'heaven lies about us in our infancy'. Thomas Traherne remembered being 'entertained like an angel' when 'all time was eternity' and 'knowledge was divine'.

For Dylan Thomas, his childhood companions in 'Fern Hill' were 'Adam and maiden'. 'So it must have been,' he reflected, 'after the birth of the simple light in the first spinning place ...'

In his poem 'The Retreat', Henry Vaughan's hope is that 'when this dust falls to the urn / In that state I came, return'.

In one of his moving reflections, theologian Karl Rahner offers a more hopeful point of view. He holds that our childhood is not the elusive mirage of an unattainable heaven, a moment to be lived through and lost forever. It is, rather, each human being's potential for beatitude, in this life and the next. Paradoxical as it may seem, we grow into the fullness of the childhood we once lived through. For him, the gifts and graces of our early years are the clearest and closest expression of God's incarnate nature – and of our unaware and partial participation in it. He reflects on the child's unknowing familiarity with the mystery that is denied to 'the wise and clever'. Is this not why Jesus summed up his teaching about the kingdom of heaven in the vibrant symbol of a child?

Rahner takes us an astonishing step further. He is convinced that this childhood is what we fully recover, completely possess, and ultimately freely celebrate in the playgrounds of heaven. 'We do not move away from childhood in any real sense,' he writes. 'We move towards the eternity of this childhood, to its definitive and enduring validity in God's sight – a field which bears fair flowers and ripe fruits such as can grow in this field of childhood, and no other, and which will be carried into the storehouses of eternity.'

Some people grow like a tree grows. A tree never loses the integral, authentic shape of itself. Like the child, the tree does not want to be anybody or anything else. It only wants to become more fully what it already is. It is in this 'being true to themselves' that people most resemble and worship God. In his poem 'The Bright Field' ('of great price') R. S. Thomas reflects this vision:

> ... It is the turning
> aside like Moses to the miracle
> of the lit bush, to a brightness
> that seemed as transitory as your youth
> once, but is the eternity that awaits you.

There are many unique qualities in our childhood state and memories, but the grace of openness flows through them all. It is openness that allows wonder to steal in, and our dreams to steal out. It is in our openness, according to St Thomas Aquinas, that we most resemble God. It is a vulnerable openness, this readiness to apprehend the invisible world, this recollection of an elusive heaven almost within our grasp. Such sacramental moments of openness have an eternal edge of expectancy to them, a reaching beyond our capacities, a yearning for gifts from beyond.

John Betjeman remembers a moment of this excited anticipation. It was during a storm when the spring tide and blizzard united to force the sea to rush back up the lane near his childhood home. Warm in their waders, he and his friends waited for the wreckage of treasures to come swirling into reach. His poem 'Trebetherick' ends with a touching prayer:

> Blessed be St Enodoc, blessed be the wave,
> Blessed be the springy turf, we pray, pray to thee,
> Ask for our children all the happy days you gave,
> To Ralph, Vasey, Alastair, Biddy, John and me.

I used to ask my mother what I was like when I was small. She said I was always celebrating something, and always wanting more than my head or heart or arms could hold. She compared me to the *slua sidhe*, the invisible faery-folk of Ireland who were always searching between two worlds – the real and the really real. I was one with nature then, she reflected. I clung to the high branches of the swaying trees when the Atlantic summer winds blew magic around our house in *Sliabh Luachra*, the Valley of the Rushes. There was music everywhere for my bare and dancing feet. I must have been living then in some kind of sacramental world. Everything was new, and everything was now, and everything was forever. And that is why I wanted to be a priest. And that was before everything changed …

But still the search goes on. *Tablet* columnist Jonathan Tulloch and his wife, Shirley, wrote and recited a poem to mark my recent Golden Jubilee. The final words of 'Heaven is Seven' came to them, they said, like echoes from between two worlds:

> I will meet you
> on tomorrow's dawn
> at the crossroads of Rathmore,

at the parting of the world's ways,
and together we will wait for Father Christmas,
ice cream in Killarney,
Woodbines behind the church wall,
and the final morning's lark singing
above the field of great price.

Miracles of hope

A trip to Knock is a reminder that some unlikely places act as repositories of memories or associations. In them, it seems possible to transcend even the darkest hours of life and catch a glimpse of the ultimate destiny for which we were all created.

Relentlessly the rain off the sea beat down on the small fields of Mayo. On the evening of 22 August 1879, a man is passing through a tiny village in the west of Ireland. He is looking for work. A woman is having tea with her neighbour, their words heavy with anxiety. A farmer is slowly returning from his flat meadow after urgently making up the sodden hay. A few women are sheltering in the doorway of Waldron's grocery shop.

Four troubled men are huddled inside Mullen's forge fearful at the prospect of another failure of the crops – for the third consecutive year. Would the curse of the recent famine fall on the wretched people again? Suddenly someone cried out and began pointing excitedly. A strange light had started to shine from the eastern gable-end of the bleak church nearby. Everyone rushed down the broken road.

From that moment, the lives of the people of that tiny hamlet were changed forever. Because it was Our Lady herself, they believed, who had appeared, like a morning star, on that dull, depressing nightfall. Today, a million and half people visit the place every year. There is now an international airport at Knock.

My mind was full of memories and reflections recently, as I gazed at the memorabilia in the small museum beside the huge basilica. Bits and pieces of a typical tiny cottage or hut were on display – the bellows for the fire, the skillet for cooking, the candlestick and the holy water font for warding off the evil spirits. Horseshoes and an anvil from 'Old Tom' Mullen's forge were there, and items from Michael Waldron's shop including an invoice (no 26) for 8 shillings and 10 pence (reduced by a penny for prompt payment).

Every August during the Forties my mother brought us here. It was a long train journey from Kerry. We said the Rosary and sang hymns all the way up and all the way down. My Auntie Molly used to bring dozens of bottles of Cade's yellow lemonade and lashings of ham in thick wedges of home-made soda bread. Rarely was the journey without incident. I remember the blood that flowed when a wooden-framed banner ('Our Lady of Knock pray for the people of Rathmore'), stowed away on the rack over the seats, fell on Paddy Stack's bald head during the recitation of the Fifth Sorrowful Mystery. When we finally arrived at the Place of Apparition people thought we were bringing this severely bandaged patient to Knock for 'the cure'.

Everything in that museum stirred memories and told stories – stories of real poverty and the desperate struggle for survival. It was a bad time for Ireland. Crushed by the famine and foreign rule, its heart was barely beating. Why here, and why now, did that most astonishing event take place? What kind of heavenly mind, I wondered, would choose this most grim and desolate place as the setting for the revelation of the most sublime and spiritual beauty? And why are millions drawn there every year to ponder its mysterious history?

There is a hidden passion in people for signs of transcendence even against all the odds. From all time, and in all cultures and religions, people carry within them a dogged belief in an ultimate meaning, a hope for what is beyond – and within. We all share a sense of belonging to something greater in the universal human journey. When we walk and pray in those timeless places of divine disclosure, our steps resonate with those of people before us, our words echo an unconscious and archetypal solidarity with all valiant pilgrims. When we sing the hymns, hold the candles of faith, and chant the rosaries of our beliefs, we are refusing to give in to the existential temptation to despair. Barefoot on the cold stones of Connacht, and hungry in its slanting rain, even as children, we were being reminded of another destiny. We were part of a bigger story, moments in a grander drama. Our lives did not begin with our birth. Our parents, our grandparents, all our ancestors were protecting that small light within us, to keep at bay those demons of nihilism that suddenly shadow the faint glimmerings of the hope we cling on to.

Knock – and all such places of possibility – encapsulate the shifting seasons of the human and divine soul. They are the world in microcosm, the universal pilgrimage in miniature.

They are open to all who are searching for a meaning, an identity, a reason for hoping. They ask for no spiritual passport, no certificate of worthiness, no official invitation, no annulment of past mistakes. If you are hungry the table is set for you; if your wounded heart is ready, it will be healed. They are places where we are all equal, where, despite our current dark doubts, heaven is believed to exist and is open to all.

Do we return again and again to such places because our often desperate need to find a reason for living is no longer recognised on the Sundays of our mainstream churches? Maybe our deepest desires for new beginnings find an echo in the eternal innocence, immortalised in the human woman of the apparitions where children and the poor are usually the seers. Do we see them as precious reminders of the divine child in ourselves, of the original vision we were born with, of the kindly light we strain to glimpse, of the ultimate destiny for which we were created?

These glimpses of heaven are never confined to one story, one moment, one church. True Catholic sacramentality knows no containment, confinement or regulated outlets. The mystery is all too deep, too sensitive, too fragile for any controlling systems. It transcends religion. It is intrinsic to Creation and humanity. And just about anything to which we are truly present can be the sacramental moment that calls and lifts us to the vision of our divine source and destiny.

For some this moment will be the glimpse of a ladybird on a leaf, a tear in a child's eye, the sound of earth on the lid of a coffin. For others it will be the miracle of a birth in a dead place or a patch of light on a dismal wall. For others still it will be the personal and cosmic power revealed in a broken piece of bread. And whether in Knock or Auschwitz the miracles of hope will continue to happen.

'The misery here is quite terrible,' wrote Etty Hillesum in her last concentration camp diary entry, 'and yet, late at night when the day has slunk away into the deaths behind me, I often walk along the barbed wire. And then, time and time again, it soars straight from my heart – I can't help it, that's just the way it is, like some elementary force – the feeling that life is glorious and magnificent, and that one day we shall be building a whole new world.'

On not being good enough

It is our fear-driven ego that makes us try too hard to give the impossible 110 per cent. How much better it is sometimes just to be grounded in God.

From the front door of the great hall on top of an Oakland hill we had a stunning view of San Francisco Bay. Inside the hall, however, things were not so pleasant. About 80 of us were gathered at one end while our director slowly called out a list of negative attitudes that were seen as blockages to the flow of life and love within us. As the name of each shadow was announced, those who identified with it moved across the floor to the far side.

It was a kind of healing, penitential ritual, part of a long retreat to do with identifying the personal shadows that, in the words of St Paul, prevented our 'hidden self' from growing strong. The usual seven deadly sins each brought one or two retreatants to their feet – to begin their short, exposed journey. When, however, 'feeling not good enough' was called out, a whole crowd of us lumbered across the great hall in embarrassment, but feeling some kind of comfort in numbers, too.

In my pastoral experience a common cry from those seeking a fuller life concerns the inbuilt sense of inferiority and the fear of being judged. That is why we pretend and tell lies; it is why we try to impress in a thousand ways; it lies at the heart of untold misery and even tragedy. Whether in the least competitive of small communities, or at the heady heights of political or religious power, you will find the silent fear of failure, the watchful tensions at the precarious edge of peer-comparison.

This subtle feeling of inadequacy steals in everywhere. Last year I was helping the parish priest at the celebration of First Reconciliation on an evening where all the concerned adults – parents, teachers and catechists – were gathered informally in the one space before the altar. The well-prepared young sinners, at first waiting patiently for their turn, gradually sensed that no one was 'in charge'. They had a field day! Each group of adults was reluctant to take control of the situation, I heard later. They felt that the children might publicly disobey and embarrass them. Rather than risk being seen as 'not good enough', they pretended not to notice the growing chaos.

The world-renowned leader in psychoanalysis and child psychiatry, D. W. Winnicott, introduced the phrase 'good enough mothers' as a way of reassuring them that they do not have to be perfect mothers. He urged them to trust their own love for their children, their own natural instincts. This guidance must come as a great relief to so many parents who push themselves beyond their limits, who try too hard, who think that only 100 per cent will do. There is a liberating wisdom in being allowed to get down off the daily competitive edge of a relentless drive to prove competency.

It is the fear-driven ego that makes us strive too hard – to give more than we are capable of because we do not believe that even our best is ever 'good enough'. We can too easily get in the way of the flow and dance of life when we try too hard. But we do not have to do it all. We keep forgetting that there is an undercurrent of divinity in our lives that shapes, guides and empowers everything. We are called to, fashioned for, drawn towards, knowingly or not, an infinite destiny.

'In each baby is a vital spark, and this urge towards life and growth and development is a part of the baby, something the baby is born with, and which is carried forward in a way we do not have to understand,' says Winnicott, who is maybe urging the mother to leave room for God in the baby's life, to allow a space for the baby to just 'be' – a space where the baby ultimately develops a sense of a separate 'self'. To be grounded in the 'hidden self' is, in a way, to be grounded in God. Maybe God is at one and the same time both the space and the spark and the self. But never the worry.

Whether our complexes tend towards inferiority or superiority, the roots of them can be traced to early childhood experiences. We drink in our mother's anxiety with her milk, we absorb our father's desperate striving through our pores. At the recent National Conference of Priests, David Wells told us about the retirement party of an extremely talented and hugely successful head teacher. When the crowds had gone home, a few people stayed on to clean up the hall and stack the tables. With a deep, weary sigh the highly acclaimed leader loosened his tie, undid the top button of his shirt, slumped into a chair and whispered, 'Well, they can't get me now.'

In *A New Earth* Eckhart Tolle writes: 'Be alert. Are some of the thoughts that go through your mind the internalised thoughts of your father or mother saying perhaps something like, "You are not good enough. You will never amount to anything" or some other judgement or mental position? If there is awareness in you, you will be able to recognise that voice in your head for what it is: an old thought conditioned by the past; an old thought – no more. This awareness dissolves the unconscious past in you.'

Otherwise our pain continues. We suffer by way of inner doubt and often depression; we lose our personal charisma, courage and inner peace. The joy of Being leaves our lives. Our gifts remain unused – and something unique remains for ever unborn. Our lack of self-belief leaves its mark on our minds, souls and bodies. Internalised self-doubt eventually affects our health. When it impacts on our appearance we are tempted by the excesses of dieting, makeovers and cosmetic surgery. We no longer sense that Presence within – from which all true beauty shines. Without a healthy sense of self we project our unhappiness outwards. As our harsh treatment of ourselves sets in, so does our dismissiveness and cynicism about others. We begin to see the world through the filter of our own complexes. I remember an evening of impromptu entertainment in a former parish. Someone was needed to play the piano. When an unlikely looking, rather portly volunteer ambled towards the gap-toothed keyboard on a makeshift stage there were some doubtful, if not judgemental, expressions and comments from those around me. Let Anna Wigley's 'The Jazz Pianist' describe what happened next:

> Before he sits at the keys he seems
> short-breathed with bulk:
> his belly a whale, his arms fat fish
> that struggle to hang straight.
> He takes the slender stool between his legs
> and perches; a buffalo on a shooting-stick.
> The hands come up and rest
> over the keys in dainty readiness.
> Then he pulls from the piano's throat
> with such a deft, exquisite touch
> brilliant scarves; and we stare
> as if the room were full of strange weather.

Alternative healing

New Age spirituality has been condemned by a variety of voices in the church, but it would be wrong to reject its enthusiasts out of hand. Their spiritual longing, like that of many Christians, is to try their best to find the still centre at the universal heart of love.

In Dublin for a weekend analysing the meaning and discussing the healing power of dreams I overheard a woman on her way to Mass. Seeing the notice outside the church hall proclaiming 'Wake up to Your Dreams,' she remarked to her companion in a delightful accent, 'Dre-ams, dre-ams,' she said. 'Didn't the Pope ban dem?'

From time to time, and especially in recent years, rumblings of discontent have been heard down the corridors of the Vatican regarding various popular healing practices. Beyond the analysis of dreams, the finger of hierarchical suspicion has been pointed at acupuncture, the Enneagram, centring prayer and reiki. In August a leader in *The Times* quoted a Catholic priest who believed that 'an evil spirit tries to make his entry' through yoga.

People are genuinely and continually confused by these recurring rumours of hidden and dangerous forces. Some denunciations are the hysterical tirades of fundamentalist evangelicals; others are the understandable concerns of anxious believers. At any rate, in spiritual centres up and down those countries where such holistic sessions are regularly offered, I'm often asked about their 'standing in the Catholic Church'. Are they safe? Are they from God? Are they New Age?

There are, of course, perverse aberrations to be found in many New Age spiritualities – providing wide targets for the Christian Right. But wild scapegoating and labelling is an old and clever trick of church and state to protect the *status quo*. Yet surprisingly, while loosely eclectic, much New Age enthusiasm can be traced to Christian roots. And many traditions of Christianity have their origins in pagan rituals. It is not the way of Jesus to marshal the battle lines too soon.

A great deal of 'establishment' fear often stems from a flawed grasp of a theology of sin and redemption where the human becomes a threat to the holy, where the body seduces the soul, where grace is not at home in the physical, where divine healing is separated off from its human enfleshment. But, for the truly orthodox Christian all healing, whether explicitly recognised or not, is God's unique gift. To deny humanity its redeeming power must be the ultimate heresy.

While studying in San Francisco, I agreed to meet and share with groups of New Age adherents. These exchanges were mostly mutually enriching. It was challenging work in that New Agers have neither a creed nor a formal organisation to focus on. Yet we were able to explore common ground about the beauty of creation, about our universal co-responsibility for care of the earth, about the divine energy everywhere, about the inter-connectedness of all things, about Christian humanism and about a theology of creation.

In the 1990s the subject of New Age beliefs and practices was addressed by the Vatican in its document, *Jesus Christ the Bearer of the Water of Life*. It outlined the positive dimensions of many of these New Age movements but condemned many of its basic tenets as 'Godless and without merit'. Yet throughout there was a clear reminder for Catholics to pay attention to these 'signs of the times', calling Christians themselves to a necessary reformation in the light of the gospel.

During my time with New Agers we tried to build wide bridges at our closest points rather than argue at our points of greatest divergence. We attempted to name some New Age aspirations in Christian terms, where, for example, in a human Saviour, many of their yearnings were already purified and revealed; where the essential meaning of what they addressed as 'life-energy' or 'universal consciousness' was earthed in time and space in Christian incarnation. In this very context Pope John Paul II remarked that 'here too there is an Areopagus to be evangelised'.

Such a bridge, we felt, was gradually being built, a bridge over which the best of what they already believed was safely carried. It was a two-way process of translation. New Age thinking, we agreed, could help Catholics rediscover the richness of their own tradition, the doctrine of Christ the Logos, the immanence of God, the sacramental imagination. While agreeing with the thrust of the Vatican summary, Cardinal Godfried Danneels admitted that New Age criticism of the church has a point with respect to a Catholic lack of emphasis on lived experience, its fear of mysticism, its endless exhortations, its over-insistence on the primacy of doctrine.

There was another vital moment in our dialogue. Many New Agers were confused and disillusioned about their failure to transform themselves into deeper levels of being. 'Why,' they asked, 'was it so difficult?' Exercises were followed, affirmations made, the Mystery invoked, the circles formed. But something was not working.

It was then that we talked about the Christian understanding of the power and stubbornness of the ego, the human attraction to darkness as well as to the light, the strong inclination to evil in all of us, the congenital blindness that no amount of self-induced consciousness will ever eradicate. We found ourselves exploring this shadowland called original sin, and a tough Christian theology of the Cross, to understand the graced process of human transformation. Much as a postmodern world may desire it, humanity can never be the agent of its own salvation.

True Christianity has always reverenced the ready soil of the human spirit as the graced ground for the seeds of God. It is God who has placed the restless longing in the hearts of millions of New Age men and women yearning for the personal and universal 'abundant life'. Whether it be regarding reiki, dreams, yoga or Enneagram work, when the intentions of those involved are truly spiritual, then it is here that God is becoming incarnate again. It is therefore such a pity when we, as church, approach these hidden graces with the dull gleam of disapproval in our eyes.

Who is foolish enough to pronounce as 'Godless' the inner sanctuary of those sensitive people who yearn for a new age of peace? And who is so rash as to pass judgement on those beloved daughters and sons of a Parent God who, in their own way, are seeking an intimacy with the Mystery before which they stand in wonder? The very human core of such spiritual longing is already a tender incarnation of the divine imagination.

Such genuine people may, like the rest of us, often lose their way, but are simply trying their best to make their lives and the world more beautiful, to find the still centre of the universal heart of love. In Sydney this summer Pope Benedict XVI spoke of the 'yearning, universal, human cry to be immersed in communion'. We need to remember that.

Don't forget to wake early

If we are in a state of depression, or prone to such states, it is at least partly our habits of thought that bring us there or keep us there. But, even on the dark winter mornings, it is possible to allow ourselves to emerge from the gloom.

'Night and day my thoughts are driving me mad. Nor can I pray anymore.' Such anxious cries are becoming more common in our parishes and communities. Few people today are untouched by the temptation to chronic unhappiness, to depression, to despair. And bleak winter days are no help to such victims of the mind when that temptation comes.

It is suggested by many that in our quiet desperation we try too hard to free our mind from such thoughts. We panic at our inability to shift the anxiety we have compulsively built within us. We storm heaven and start novenas. But the more we try the worse it gets. By putting relentless pressure on our minds we only spin the vicious circle faster. All we are mostly doing, the experts tell us, is reinforcing the patterns of thinking that keep activating our pain. Through a deep, existential fear, perhaps, or a pessimistic turn of mind, we exaggerate the negative, we falsely fantasise about the distressing outcome of things. And we take these distorted thoughts as the absolute truth.

These thoughts then trap us, turning a small sadness into a web of anxiety. A harmless event, a throwaway comment can escalate into a flood of depressing emotions that destroy our sense of worthiness and joy. Our very thinking becomes the enemy, according to writers Eckhart Tolle and Richard Rohr. Most of it (85 per cent, they claim) serves only to upset us more. The Irish poet and philosopher John O'Donohue refers to the 'crippling effect of our dried-out, dead thoughts in the cul-de-sac of our lives'. Our incessant, defeatist focusing on things that happen to us ties us into an even tighter tangle.

A helpful beginning is the understanding that it is not the facts themselves that bring on depressive attitudes, but how our minds deal with those facts. Our habitual reaction to a passing disappointment can transform it into a persistent, unsettling unhappiness. Like a blind automatic pilot, our warped thinking becomes seriously misleading. Our contact with life, with the truth, is no longer a direct or reliable one.

In *The Mindful Way Through Depression* authors Williams, Teasdale, Segal and Kabat-Zinn offer a different approach to improving the quality of our lives by practising another way of thinking – a combination of an Eastern meditative tradition and Western cognitive therapy. They ask us to replace the 'doing mode' of the mind with the 'being mode'. Instead of allowing ourselves to be seduced into unhappiness by our false and toxic thinking, or our fearful efforts to avoid or suppress emotions – maybe around persistent memories of a long-past humiliation, an imagined fear, or a grief that has lost its way – it is possible to directly encounter and experience those thoughts without the depressing fabrications we weave around them.

'Mindfulness' is how they describe this process of dealing only with the reality of present experiences rather than linking them with past failures, real or imaginary. The secret is to become aware of ourselves thinking and feeling. This new hygiene of the mind does not fight with or try to banish 'the enemy within'; rather it befriends those threatening thoughts and moods, carefully exploring them realistically with a non-judgemental compassion – but eternally vigilant for their deadly tricks, traps and temptations.

It is in this watchful silence, Henri Nouwen believes, that we can recognise the ways we try to hide and avoid facing the truth about ourselves; the way we can come to distinguish the reality of our condition from the irrational scenario of alarm, disgrace or self-blame that we fearfully attach to it. He pictures our fears and panic as emerging from where we have hidden them, and saying to us, 'You can only be free if you look at us in the face. We are not as awful as you imagine. When you see us as we really are, not as you think we are, you will be free to find your happiness again.'

In the 'being mode' we experience and embrace the objective reality of what is unfolding around us. We acknowledge the way things are, without any mental fencing or forcing. Mindfulness is about paying non-judgemental attention only to what is actually happening at any given moment; not to the fearful anticipation, the false stories, the depressing possibilities that something compulsive inside us wildly weaves as true.

This type of awareness is much more than paying attention

with more concentration; it is about how we pay attention. As if standing behind a waterfall, we calmly observe the cascade of our mental distortions without getting dragged down, like defenceless victims, into the pool of depression.

We need to keep reminding ourselves that our unmindful thoughts are passing mental events. They are not reality itself. We must harvest the precious energy of our mind for the current task in hand – to see things as they are, not as we are. Dr Raj Persaud, senior lecturer in psychiatry at the University of London, traces our inner distress to an inability to 'keep our thoughts and emotions current', to adapt them coherently to the actual changes in our circumstances.

Under the Spirit, a healthy mind will draw the hidden self towards the abundant life. The free and present mind beckons us on ever-new journeys – to feel and fulfil our longing for joy, to bring beckoning horizons within our reach. But the predetermined tramlines of yesterday's dark thinking will not bring us to places of hope or imagination. The Irish poet Patrick Kavanagh wrote, 'To be dead is to stop believing in the masterpieces we will begin tomorrow.'

'Mind your mind,' O'Donohue reminds us. We are all responsible for our own thoughts. We have the spiritual power to choose joy, to respond with gratitude even on a grey day, to think in happier rhythms. The beautiful, fragile mind is the place of our most profound freedom. That is why, in all its wanderings, obsessions and struggles, it must be nourished, cherished and protected. In the purifying of our mind it is important, the wise tell us, to keep constantly grounded in our own bodies and in the energy of the earth.

For many, these dark, winter mornings are the hardest times. Yet, with courage, with dedicated practice, we can welcome each day like a child waking up with a new look in her eyes, blessing with delight everything she looks at, praising God unknowingly for everything she touches. She is the small baptismal priestess within us, presiding at the table of each fresh beginning, consecrating again the bread and wine of our morning minds. 'And don't forget to awake early,' the Sufi poet Rumi reminds us. 'The breeze at dawn has secrets to tell you. Do not go back to sleep; do not go back to sleep.'

Autumn song

It is the mellow season, a time to reflect on those things that have grown, flourished and faded during the year, and, more importantly, those that remain with us – the fixed melodies of our life – to carry us through the cold of winter to the promise of spring.

With autumn's perennial intimations of endings, many feel drawn to reflect more profoundly on one or other dimension of the mystery of their lives.

This October, the aspect that keeps coming back to me concerns the nature of my innermost conviction, my fundamental motivation, the constant logo of my soul that sums up my reason for living. What, in essence, is the bare, core focus that sustains me when all else falls away?

I have just finished Michael Mayne's *The Enduring Melody*. This, too, has stimulated my search for what nourishes my soul in times of spiritual famine. The author, who was slowly and painfully dying while writing this rich and recent book, explored what he called the *cantus firmus* that underpinned his life – the fixed song, the plainchant cadence unadorned by harmony or counterpoint. During the time of our lives many notes will weave their way in and out and around the steadfast refrain, but the basic melody endures. There's always a bit of firm ground that never alters.

It is when we find age, autumn or death upon us that we begin to think about what has remained constant throughout the vicissitudes of our lives; what has offered the persistent direction to a 'north' for the compass of our souls. Is there any musical echo within us about which we can say, with Mayne, 'this has been mine, and mine alone: however much I have deviated from it and chosen my own note-lengths, this is its ground bass. There are certain critical truths and experiences that have seized and shaped me, and it is this firm ground that speaks to me of what is authentic, and to which I can return, touching base, as it were, at every stage of my unpredictable human journey'?

Looking at the unswerving conviction in the lives of people we admire may help us to reach that precious place in our own hearts. The persistence of Mahatma Gandhi, for instance, in the pursuit of his vision, was nurtured by his utter conviction of the equality of all people. He never gave up because the *cantus firmus* for ever played this refrain in his soul: 'God is to be found in the next person you meet, or not at all.'

In spite of huge disappointments in her life, my own mother's fierce faith in the ultimate goodness of God was frightening in its certainty. It saw her through many a bleak midwinter. Jesus himself, exhausted from his temptations and despairing during his temporary loss of faith on the Cross, never completely lost the persistent reassurance of his loving intimacy with his Father. That was his *cantus firmus*, the guardian angel of God that sang to his often confused soul. In light of recent confessions and revelations about the faith (or lack of it) in the life of Mother Teresa, we can only wonder at length about the nature of the 'fixed song' that kept her motivated though she could not hear it.

Not long before he died earlier this year, the Kerry mystic and scholar John Moriarty wrote: 'Clear days bring the mountains down to my doorstep; calm nights give the rivers their say; the wind puts its hand on my shoulders some evenings, and then I stop thinking. I just leave what I'm doing and I go the soul's way.' For many, an extraordinary affinity with nature would be the enduring melody that always brings the solace, the healing, the enthusiasm to continue along 'the soul's way', or maybe even to start the long journey again.

Not long before he was killed by the Nazis, Dietrich Bonhoeffer wrote *Letters and Papers from Prison*. Michael Mayne quotes him: 'God requires that we should love him eternally with our whole hearts, yet not so as to compromise or diminish our earthly affections, but as a kind of *cantus firmus* to which the other melodies of life provide the counterpoint … Where the ground bass is firm and clear, there is nothing to stop the counterpoint from being developed to the utmost of limits. Only a polyphony of this kind can give life a wholeness, and assure us that nothing can go wrong so long as the *cantus firmus* is kept going … Put your faith in the *cantus firmus*.'

The truth that lived at the heart of Michael Mayne's own life, tempered and polished over the decades, was his rich and colourful understanding of the Incarnation, of God's selfportrait in Jesus. It was because of his sacramental vision that he could be compared to one of 'God's spies', forever picking up clues about his Creator's beauty hidden in the ordinariness of things. He believed that if we knew how to look, everything we see is touched by wonder. This very looking is, in fact, an act of transforming attention, by which, bit by bit, the world is redeemed. He quotes one of Rilke's 'Love Poems to God': 'My looking ripens things and they come towards me, to meet and be met.'

People such as Mayne, whose *cantus firmus* is the song of God as sung by the earth, are always nourishing their capacity for wonder through the work of artists. The poets, the painters, the dancers – these are the midwives of the mystery of the Presence that lives within creation and its peoples. They assure us that the experience of life is the experience of the divine. 'Make humanity your goal,' wrote St Augustine, 'and you will find your way to God.'

To take but one artist, Vincent Van Gogh, we do not have to search far to find the basic canvas of his troubled but uniquely gifted life. His most fundamental brushstrokes were drawn from his passionate belief in the inner light that radiates from everything. His *cantus firmus*, too, was based on the sacramental vision arising from the astonishing mystery of Incarnation. He wrote that he wanted to paint things 'with that something of the eternal which the halo used to symbolise, but which we now seek to counter through the actual radiance of colour vibration'.

'The artistic works of Vincent remain behind like sacraments,' writes Benedictine monk Mark Patrick Hederman, 'revealing to those who have eyes to see this new sense and symbolism with which he incarnated the mystery of the presence of God in our world. His paintings are liturgies which unfold the mysteries of God's presence in our day-to-day world, more powerfully, perhaps, than any written word can do.'

Having said all of this, there are moments, however, when our lifelong lifelines of faith and support seem to let us down. Picked clean of all ambiguity and honed to essential truth, even our most tried and trusted mantras of meaning will lose their power to motivate our stalling spirit. The eternal refrain, the fixed song, the enduring melody have grown silent.

These are the times when the only *cantus firmus* left to us to fall back on may well be the most unnoticed, but most fiercely faithful and graced melody of all: the reliable rhythm of our own breathing and the bright beating of our own heart.

Naturally blessed

Every blessing is a reminder of the original blessing – that of life itself. To administer one is to divine a wellspring of sacred presence, already secure below the surface of everything – and in that lies the true meaning of Incarnation.

October in North Yorkshire. We were gathered in the parish school for our Autumn Mass of the Sick. The St Vincent de Paul Society stalwarts, who lovingly prepare these popular Eucharists, had begun with their children the custom of blessing each needy parishioner as I moved around anointing them. Before this particular celebration, we had wondered about asking those same parishioners to bless us as well. We were a little anxious. Some in our team thought it might be too big a challenge.

We need not have feared. With an unaffected elegance, the ill, the elderly, leant forward from their seats and wheelchairs, and graciously and smilingly placed their hands on our heads and shoulders, murmuring words of healing and comfort. It was as though they were only waiting to be asked, as though this was something they had always wished to do. Blessing came naturally to them.

Liturgical purists may have some problems with such heartfelt moments of grace and blessing. But that afternoon there was an unforgettable atmosphere of divine presence, when we, the so-called able-bodied, knelt for the healing touch of those we were serving. Both diminished and empowered by their pain, they were the *anawim* in whom God's own essence burnt most fiercely. Here, in the shadow of their Cross, was the primary source of divine blessing.

Those trembling, gnarled human hands that were reaching out to touch us were alive with grace. They were small sacraments of the compassion of the incarnate God. They were beautiful in their long history of caring and comforting, of failing and falling, of nourishing and nurturing. They had proved their worthiness. That is why they were fashioned for blessing, too, for calling out the image of God from every broken heart, for resurrecting divine courage where only weakness now lived.

Surely it is a lovely aspect of baptism, for instance, to see it as a thanksgiving blessing for the birth of the baby, already blazing with God's glory, but also vulnerable to losing it in the encounter with the waiting 'sin of the world'? Instead of seeing the baby's life as only really beginning at the font, how delightful it is to see the sacrament as the recognition of the divine image already fresh and shining in that baby from birth, and now so warmly embraced into the family of Jesus.

Towards the end of the celebration, I usually invite the oldest grandparent to bless the baby. The spontaneous and natural way they do this, protecting God's dream in the little one, blessing her with their wisdom for the thresholds and transitions awaiting her, always takes my breath away. And through her life, when that baby continues to be blessed by her parents with the sign of the Cross every morning and night, blessed by her friends and her own senses, blessed by the prayers and sacraments of the church, she will be reminded again and again, particularly during the winters of her life, of the Original Blessing that her life is from the beginning. To be born is to be chosen and blessed.

Anticipating similar sentiments in John Paul II's eucharistic writings, Fr Antonio Rosmini, philosopher and founder of the Institute of Charity, had a profound sense of the Mass as a permanent blessing within the earth. He sees that blessing as the releasing of all the seeds for good and for love implanted by God at the core of everything. Eucharistic celebration blesses and stirs that implanted impulse so that these seeds are confirmed and nourished to blossom to their divine potential. 'All things in this world, animate and inanimate', he wrote, 'are [revealed as] sanctified by the Body and Blood consecrated by the priest.'

As priests what are we doing when we bless? Are we actually making something holy, adding on something that was missing, spiritually disinfecting a merely natural object? Or are we revealing a hidden richness, divining a wellspring of sacred presence, already secure below the surface of everything? Is this not the true meaning of Incarnation?

Is consecrated ground more sacred than the kitchen floor burnished and blessed by the feet of the families who played and prayed on it? We take off our shoes because all ground is holy ground. We bless the land to reveal that every bush is a burning bush. Is the still water in the church font holier than the dancing water in the stream nearby? We bless water to invoke, enhance and reveal its ageless, unique and beautiful healing power.

In his *Blessing – A Theology of Creation?* Canon Alan Griffiths writes: 'The tradition of blessing *for* something rather than *upon* something, as though (holiness) were not already there, has echoes in the theology that underpinned Vatican II and its understanding of grace. Karl Rahner held that the sacramental event brings grace to expression without denying its pre-existence. Grace is always there: the sacraments do not supply it but express it. They reveal its presence ...'

Everyone can bless. It comes with our already-graced humanity. There are people who can be called sacraments of blessing. There are those whose hands, eyes and bodies are always blessing everyone and everything around them. But not all are like that. Take the example of the graceless tone of current exchanges in internet blogs. In our confused church today there are many strong convictions. But some are expressed with a reckless disregard for people's feelings. They carry no blessing. According to a recent report from the Evangelical Alliance, church leaders find Christian blogs the most hurtful of all. In a Hasidic saying we read, 'Rake the muck this way, rake the muck that way, it will still be muck. Wouldn't you be better off spreading blessings on your way to heaven?'

Friends (and enemies) probably have no idea of the eternal effect they have on each other. There is a memory in every blessing that remains hidden in the warp and weft of our souls. Fresh within me still is the Celtic blessing my mother left on my pillow the night before I left home for the first time:

Be thine the encompassing of the God of life;
Be thine the encompassing of the Christ of love;
Be thine the encompassing of the Spirit of grace;
To befriend thee and to aid thee,
O Donal, beloved of my breast:
To befriend thee and to aid thee,
Thou beloved of my heart.

After many a summer

For us, as we now are, everything passes. In particular, we have to say goodbye at some point to those people we love most and those places to which we are most deeply attached. The emotions associated with this essential aspect of our humanity are deep and complex.

October has a melancholy edge, with its shadow of endings, loss and death that perennially disturbs our deepest spirit. It is during this month that we are most likely to experience a subtle and powerful emotion called 'pathos'. Pathos carries a special kind of ache. It is tinged with sadness, longing and loss.

The inevitable passing of things has a piercing poignancy. A moment comes when we are moved beyond measure at the awful truth that nothing is permanent. In *Glimpses of Eden* Jonathan Tulloch recently wrote about one such moment. He perceived 'the gathering of the swallows' in autumn as the harbinger of deeper transitions.

Eoinín na nÉan (Little Owen of the Swallows) was dying. No one knew why. One autumn day he told his mother that he would be leaving this earth with the imminent departure of his flying friends. The local people sensed a strange bond between the boy and the birds. It was a still evening when Eoinín was sitting on some rocks near his home.

As the wheeling swallows fell into formation for their long journey to brighter places, they paused for a trembling moment of pure being, before swooping up and away to distant shores. It was then that one of them swung round, back and down, the story goes, and brushed with its wing, a big tear from the small pale face. His bewildered mother, watching from behind the curtains, was weeping too.

The power of pathos releases the hidden tears of things, the *lacrimae rerum* of the philosophers and mystics. Irish patriot and poet Pádraig Pearse evokes a tender empathy in us with these lines from *The Wayfarer*:

> The beauty of the world hath made me sad,
> This beauty that will pass;
> Sometimes my heart hath shaken with great joy
> To see a leaping squirrel on a tree,

Or a red ladybird upon a stalk,
Or little rabbits in a field at evening,
Lit by a slanting sun ...
And I have gone upon my way
Sorrowful.

'Michael' is one of Wordsworth's powerful pathetic poems.
Michael and his wife eke out a living on a small farm and deeply
love their only son. The day comes when he must leave them to
find work abroad. He falls into bad company and never returns
home. At this point, Noel Dermot O'Donoghue points out in his
book *Heaven in Ordinarie* that the sorrow and sympathy we now
feel is not yet pathos. Pathos enters in when the poet tells the
story of the sheep-fold that Michael and his son had just begun
to build together.

... Lay now the corner-stone,
As I requested; and hereafter, Luke,
When thou art gone away, should evil men
Be thy companions, think of me, my son,
And of this moment ... Now fare thee well –
When thou returnest, thou in this place will see
A work not yet here; a covenant
'Twill be between us – ...

Lovingly the old man attended daily to the task of building
this stone pledge of a longed-for reunion. One day the bad news
came. The prodigal son would never return. Nor would his father
ever recover a reason for living.

...'Tis not forgotten yet
The pity which was then in every heart
For the old man – and 'tis believed by all
That many and many a day he thither went
And never lifted up a single stone.

What Michael feels is pure grief, maybe despair. It is the
neighbours, and we, attentive observers, who feel the pathos.
When we unexpectedly come across something that a departed
friend had loved to wear we are momentarily pierced with a
helpless, hopeless sensation of something almost indescribable.
Vincent van Gogh painted a pair of old misshapen boots. Many

of the observations of geniuses such as Paul Gauguin, Ken Wilber and Martin Heidegger regarding the essential meaning of this still-life masterpiece, explore the experience of pathos.

But the full pathetic depths of the picture, like mystery itself, elude all efforts to capture its strange and lasting power. In *The Dark* John McGahern tells the story of a boy who no longer admires or loves his father. One night he sits brooding by the fireside after his father has gone to bed. He sees his old man's muddy boots left awkwardly at the foot of the stairs. Something too deep for tears stirs in the boy's heart. The limits of his alienation are transcended. The way the boy's soul saw those discarded, hob-nailed boots evoked in him another way to understand his father. For us, the observers, this is a moment of pathos.

Pure pathos is never far away when we are present to the mystery of life and death, especially in the young, the vulnerable, the innocent. It was a sense of pathos that moved our parishioners one October Sunday morning when a fundraiser for Médecins sans Frontières spoke to us. In the course of his appeal he told the story of a young African mother who cycled 12 miles to the nearest makeshift surgery for help, her ailing baby securely strapped to her body. There was no one there. She waited all day. Her baby died as the shadows fell. The woman cycled the 12 miles back to her empty house, in the dead of night, her baby still snuggled to her breaking heart.

There is a memory that continually contracts my heart. It is of the morning that my dying brother Joseph, who suffered from Down's syndrome and renal dysfunction, left home for the last time, on his way to the Regional Hospital in Cork. I was standing at the front door of our house. Unable to ask a question, or understand what was happening to him, he looked out of the back window of the car as it left the yard. His little, lonesome, tearful face was full of confusion and fear, sensing yet more suffering for his poor bruised body, yet trying to trust those who loved him with all their hearts. Joseph returned a few days later to be waked at home. As my grief fades, the pathos grows.

The crossing-over of ending, leaving, letting go and dying are fragile, two-way thresholds. Something bleeds in life's soul when partings are forced in brutal ways. We hack ruthlessly at the delicate weft that God has woven between us. It is God's own tears we feel within us in our moments of pathos. We need to find careful and beautiful ways to say goodbye. In 'It Takes Time' in her anthology *When Leaf and Note are Gone* I. M. Birtwistle pleads:

If, when we next meet
My lips alight a butterfly on yours,
Do not cast me aside –
Old ways take time to overcome.

If, when we next meet,
I should hold your eyes too long in mine,
Have patience, I seek a lost reflection –
Love takes time to overcome.

Winter:
The Grace of Believing

When the soul dances

Instead of being drugged and drained by relentless routine, we should sway to the present music of each new day and reconnect with the essence that we all share together.

It is a great darkness when the graced light of a fresh start is threatened. That deliberate darkness, whether from within or without, is a definition of sin – whatever obscures and obstructs the flow, fling and flight of the Holy Spirit who loves to blow away from our heart everything that threatens its holy beating. We meditate early in the morning so as to allow the rhythmic Presence to freely move through our cluttered minds, still confused by the shadows of the night.

Each daybreak there is a timing and a balance to find as we set out again into another episode of the mystery of our lives. What happened to me that morning wasn't exactly the ideal way to step out into another glad day. It was a blocking, a stopping, a closing down, as though the source of my energy had been switched off. I began to realise more acutely how delicate a thing it is, the flickering light we carry.

Writing about how we begin the dance of the new day, the poet David Whyte writes: 'We should apprentice ourselves to coming awake, treat it as a form of mastery. The threshold of waking, the entry to the day, is the musician's foot lifted to begin the beat. Miss that beat and you will have to come to a stop and start again. The dash and flair of the day comes from that foot hitting the floor after the correct, restful anticipation.'

It seems to me that for our lives to be vibrant and healthy, the shadow and light in us, the demons and angels we carry, must all be allowed their shindig in the spaces of our souls. It is good for us to jump at the chance to dance.

I had finished a pint of Guinness in Westport and was seriously and prayerfully considering having another one. At that instant of indecision I was suddenly swept off the barstool and on to the floor of a set-dance. I had finished a week's conference and had little difficulty in letting go into the swing and sway of the rhythm. At regular intervals a whirling-around with three or four others took place, arms about each other's waists in a circle, to the beat of the music.

ment in their conversations than was necessary. They spoke loudly, rapidly. But the man continued dancing. And because I recognised what calling, what distant music he obeyed, I envied him.'

Jump, son! Jump!

The month of November lends itself to moods of apprehension, self-doubt and possibly despair. But there is a way through our fears – even the fear of death.

Many of us, in November, feel quite apprehensive. Something to do with our mortality. Our souls, so easily threatened, close in on themselves. We feel fragile and vulnerable. A flow dries up. An energy leaves us. Something inside us gets disconnected. As the days darken, our hearts too can lose their lightness. With the advent of winter we may notice a shift in our moods. We have long since become aware of the unpredictability of our inner peace. For many, this can be a sad and silent struggle.

We try to protect ourselves from this dark place. We learn to think carefully. We know that eternal vigilance is the key to a precarious harmony. We avoid negative people. We act happy. We try to escape into the light. None of these rather desperate pretences really works. We cannot lock ourselves into a safe mindset, building tents of bliss, as Peter wished, on a secure Mount Tabor. It is not a lasting place, the city of wine and roses. A careless forgetfulness can be like a hidden trapdoor sending us hurtling down into airless regions. And it is a long way back from those cliffs of fall.

There are times when my own spirit stalls, when the joy goes out of my days and nights. At such times, I fear sinking into the black lake of depression. Reassurances that this may be a visitation of the saintly 'dark night of the soul' bring scant consolation.

While we flounder in a sea of distress, it is difficult, at times, not to envy people who appear to have tougher minds, impervious to the subtleties of seasons, of memories and of anxieties. Their emotional lives seem more matter-of-fact and more focused on a natural kind of rhythm. They get the job done. They go out with their friends at the weekends. They laugh a lot. They love their children. They may say a few prayers and they get on with their lives. And yet – who knows what inner dramas are played out in any human heart?

I meet so many heroic people who, against all the odds, manage to keep going: the abandoned mother, shorn of her dreams, who still gets up in the morning to do what must be done for the family; the lonely old man in the retirement home who sits by the window and weakly waves at laughing children going home from school. Their hearts may be breaking, their hopes may be gone, yet something within them fuels their spirit, provides the courage they need to face each day.

As the trees turn and the leaves fall, so too do the thoughts of older people turn to our own mortality. We may fall into a melancholy tinged with loss, moist with 'the tears of things'. Across the world of cultures, November rituals grapple with the shadow of the ultimate mystery of decay and death. It is easy, at such times, to lose hope and, with it, the ability to raise ourselves to another perspective. The twin demons of fear and denial run riot in our hearts. Our horizons become too narrow, too closed. We panic. We long for a moment of breakthrough. Hacking it out piecemeal in our heads, argument by argument, brings no lasting peace. Whether that inner hell is episodic or constant, we wonder if there's an antidote for it, a lifeline to safely earth it.

Perhaps it is only at this very point of mental anguish that the miracle can happen and the paradoxical ways of God become apparent. Whatever faith means, whatever trust means, maybe they can only make sense in that awful darkness, that helpless sense of loss, that unbearable pain.

Thankfully, most of us manage to survive the ambiguous vicissitudes of our minds and hearts. Our friends encourage us, the angels draw closer, our prayers are answered and our steady patterns of being return. But there are times when a more total embracing of the darkness that engulfs our souls is called for; a more ultimate surrender of control over our lives; a more intense gathering of all our resources for a riskier leap of faith than we ever made before. This is not a noble, brave and proud capitulation, more a desperate kind of trust. Only then do we begin to sense that *point vierge* when, while it is still dark, the birds sing out their welcome, before the first rays of dawn renew the earth. It is that moment of promised clarity that brings a grounded definition to the shifting sands of our mind.

It is only when we relinquish the future into the hands of God that the fog clears and the nature of the dis-ease, the blockage within us, reveals itself. Depending on our life's choices, our age, our temperament, it will be different for each of us. What was emerging for me, this autumn, was the fact that it was the fear of my own death that confused the holy compass of my life.

Fear of death can be subtle. It darkens our days. It skews our thinking. It hangs over us threateningly – but not always consciously. It is the ghost in the wings, the ghost that reminds us of our own unpredictable exit from this world's drama. It is the ghost we all must meet before a healthy sanity returns.

The beloved Cardinal Leon Joseph Suenens told a story to help people who were blocked by their fear of dying. A fire had broken out in the middle of the night in a small two-storey house in London. All the occupants had rushed into the street to escape, except for the youngest – a four-year-old. Surrounded by dense smoke, he appeared at the upstairs window. 'Jump, my son, jump!' shouted his father. 'But Daddy I can't see you,' cried the little lad. 'Jump, son. Don't be afraid. I can see you.'

Once the fear of the final curtain is identified, encountered and, crucially, accepted (all of which does not happen on one fine day) a wonderful space is exposed and a new energy focuses our attention on present reality. All other concerns become manageable. The bigger picture brings the necessary perspective and healing. Now we can really live again, get down to the work of serving and saving our world, of reaching our destiny.

Even Jesus, deeply apprehensive before his impending death, had to unscramble his confusion, needing the clarity of his transfiguration before he set foot on the fateful road to a final Jerusalem. Advent Collects will soon remind us that the closed and fearful mind is transformed by 'the vision of wisdom', openness and light. Once we have accepted the end of our life, what's left of it may yet be the best of it. In 'The Lightest Touch', David Whyte writes:

In the silence that follows
a great line
you can feel Lazarus
deep inside
even the most deathly afraid
part of you
lift up his hands and walk toward the light.

Everywhere and nowhere

It is communication that absorbs so much time in modern life. Periods of stillness are considered a luxury, yet those times of silent contemplation connect us with the earth and with God.

For three years there was a great drought in the village. The adults were emaciated, the babies listless, the animals skeletal, the countryside desiccated. Without a harvest it had become a place of death. Then came the rumour of a Rainmaker. A last chance.

The fittest were sent out to search for him. Blessed by the gods they found him and persuaded him to return to their arid home. He listened carefully to their desperate story and then shuffled away into the local hills. After three days it began to rain. There was transformation all round. The smiles returned as bodies grew stronger, eyes began to shine as people danced to the greening of their fields. To thank the Rainmaker for his achievement, and to learn his secret should the calamity return, they searched for him again.

'No,' he said to them,]I did not make therain fall. Things were out of order in this place. There was no inner peace in the people. Nature was affected. So was I. I waited here in the valley until once again I became part of the rhythm of life. When this happened the rain fell.'

Too often we think that our inner spirit and the ways of nature are separate phenomena, that they belong to different life forces. But there is only one source of being. In his commentary on this parable, Carl Jung writes: 'When someone tells me that in his surroundings the wrong things always happen, I say, "It is you who are wrong, you are not in Tao (the path of nature) ... When one is in Tao right things happen".' In Christian terms one might refer to the cosmic Christ, to a kind of Christ consciousness, the indwelling divinity that integrates, infuses and redeems the whole of creation, awakening and reconfiguring the human psyche and the ways of the universe into the one flow of grace.

But what did the Rainmaker actually do to find this universal rhythm of being? The story goes he breathed himself into a listening stillness. Breathing and stillness. These are the contemplative spaces, he told them, in which the soul moves to the music of life in the present moment, in which authentic connections happen. It is in those spaces of connectedness that everything belongs – and the rain falls.

Breathing is the very experience of life, of being, of unity – and of God. In his *The Naked Now*, Richard Rohr OFM explains that the name and nature of God can only be breathed. The correct pronunciation of the Hebrew 'Yahweh' is an attempt to replicate and imitate the very sound of inhalation and exhalation. Notice what happens when you gently breathe in for 'Yah' and out for 'weh' a few times. It brings a sense of peace. It is the invisible life force that links all created things.

The one thing we unknowingly do every moment of our lives is therefore to speak the unifying name of God. This makes it our first and last word as we enter and leave the world. The baby arrives gasping for breath. She is gasping for life. She is gasping for God. The individual umbilical cord is broken only so that a more universal intimacy may begin. Our first breath, and every breath, brings us into deep and vital conversation with all beings and thus with the divine essence.

In our breathing we are part of a common body. We are the human lungs of God. And this experience of the sacred is open to all and sundry. It is the one precious connecting lifeline we all share. It is our common bond. There is no Islamic or Jewish way of breathing. There is no religious or secular way of breathing. As far as I know there is no special Roman Catholic way of breathing. The winds that blow across the many playing fields of God are always utterly even.

Breathing and stillness. Into what depths of stillness did the Rainmaker's breathing lead him? He retired to the hard edges of the dying village so as to be still, to be rooted in his deepest self, confident in his own truest being, secure in his own capacity for loving and being loved. For that he needed to be wholly at one with himself, stripping himself of his illusions every morning and evening of those three silent days.

'If we connect with the stillness within, we move beyond our active minds and emotions, and discover great depths of lasting peace and contentment in universal serenity,' wrote Eckhart Tolle. The Rainmaker waited so as to become fully conscious and in tune, to reconcile, in himself, like Jesus did, a disintegrating village, a fractured humanity and a splintering universe.

And only then, in his relaxed but intense awareness of his own being, and that of others, and of all Creation – only then did the rains fall. What Buddhists might call 'right relations' had been restored. What state must the human soul be in these times, when our world, our climate, our fragile balance between war and peace, is so deeply and universally out of kilter?

For many reasons stillness is a lost grace. According to Ofcom, the media regulator, the average Briton spends more than seven hours each day hooked on gadgetry. And in his just-published *The Shallows*, Nicholas Carr mourns the loss of attention and contemplation in the wake of the mind-altering technology that has come into general use. The ability to sit still, he holds, is a rare gift at a time when texting and surfing are playing havoc with our capacity for deep reflection. 'To be everywhere', wrote Seneca, 'is to be nowhere.'

In *Silence and Stillness in Every Season* John Main reminds us about the silent awareness that gives our spirit room to be free, room to breathe, saying: 'In our modern world we easily forget that we have a divine origin, a divine source, and that this unifying incandescent energy of our own spirit emanates from the Spirit of God.'

Breathing and stillness. Paradoxically, it is where the dancing happens. It is always reaching out to release a vibrant vitality in all things. 'We can make our minds so like still water', wrote W. B. Yeats, 'that beings gather about us so that they may see their own images, and so to live for a moment with a clearer, perhaps even with a fiercer life, because of our quiet.'

The great task that confronts each one of us is to discover within ourselves our own potential for creativity and unity, for reconciling in ourselves all that is splintered and separated, for allowing the original oneness of God to happen again within and around us. As it was for the Rainmaker, for all great peacemakers, for Jesus and for all of us, the truly human heart is the divine catalyst of everything that has lost its place in God's original dream for the earth. In }Navigating the Abyss to Our True Self'Thomas Merton reminds us: 'What can we gain by sailing to the moon if we are not able to cross the abyss that separates us from ourselves?'

Paradox in a manger

It is all to easy to be seduced by the season. But Christmas is not about passive peace. It causes a restlessness, a disturbance to our complacency.

A Native American warrior was rushing through the forest. He saw a fallen egg on the grass and placed it in the first nest he came across. He had placed an eagle's egg in a prairie hen's nest. One day when the hatched chickens were busy doing what a prairie-bird family does best – hopping, pecking, squawking – a magnificent eagle swooped across the sky. The young eagle was filled with a sudden, aching longing.

Immediately reprimanded by the mother hen for time-wasting and day-dreaming, the growing eagle-in-disguise dutifully continued to scratch the dry earth. But, the story goes, no matter what suspicion, ridicule or indoctrination the prairie chicken continued to endure from that day on, she could never forget that moment when her heart in hiding stirred for another bird.

As we stand around the crib something stirs inside us too. We look at the baby who will soon enjoy and endure the delights and vicissitudes of being truly human, who will later writhe in a darkness from which a great light will shine. We look at the baby and stir to an echo of heaven in ourselves.

The small child is a sign of contradiction; paradox in a manger. To be God and to be human, to be beyond and to be within, to be the future and the not yet. There is conflict, tension and pain in this graced glimpse of possibility. Like Jesus did, we carry a holy disturbance within us from birth to death. The sleepy infant holds the fullness of divine love in its finite presence and infinite promise. We kneel near the baby and an awareness of our own undreamt-of destiny awakens in us. We sense a beckoning horizon as yet invisible and uncertain. We are like people trying to remember the dream from which we have just awoken.

'Peace on earth,' we sing, but a strange disturbance bothers our hearts. 'All is calm, all is bright,' we faithfully carol, while a restlessness continues to grow within us. The perennial 'tidings of great joy' are tempered by Simeon's shadow hovering close by. 'Do you think I have come to bring peace on earth?' asked Jesus. 'No, I tell you. I have come to bring fire.'

The angels of Christmas herald in both tranquil order and troubled disorder: order in the vision of a God that has become human, of a divine dream that is happening in the land, but disorder in the blindness that blocks that dream and vision. Christmas is no passive peace. It is costly grace. God became human so that humans could become divine. This is both astonishing and upsetting. Christmas is about roots and wings. We hold within us the sublime summit, the infinite horizon to which we aspire, yet our feet of clay are rooted in the heaviness of a fallen humanity.

These echoes from another place bring a restlessness to our souls in the season of peace. This restlessness springs from the mystery of our ambiguous humanity. It is a kind of haunting by the spirits of the heavens for which we are fashioned, a perennial waking dream reminding us of the presence of a God who is always beckoning us to new summits and horizons. Referring to what he calls 'hauntings' by things beyond us, Morris West wrote: 'I am sure that it is in this domain of our daily dreaming that the Holy Spirit establishes his own communion with us. This is how the gift is given; the sudden illumination, the opening of the heart to the risk of love.'

The Christmas stories and hymns are told and sung to remind us of who we are and of who we are called to be. They are as much about us as they are about God. And we need to hear them. Otherwise we forget. Original sin obscures our inner vision and graced aspiration. It is blind to possibility. It knows nothing of summits and horizons. It travels on yesterday's flat tracks of hopeless inevitability. And yet, even though full of fear, there is always, at our core, some small stirring towards the light. There has to be. 'And the day came,' wrote Anaïs Nin, 'when the risk it took to remain tight inside the bud was more painful than the risk it took to blossom.'

Christmas disturbs adults with profound dilemmas for the soul. How do we resolve that tension between the real and the really real, that call from another place to be answered in this place? Are we open to sacrificing what we are, for what we may become? These quiet questions, all too easily stifled in the frantic lists of Christmas expectation, still carry, for the open soul, a disturbing persistence.

And all the time it is true to say that without that restless spirit, that unsatisfied longing, our desire for God would die. It is yet another dimension of the paradox of faith. The space must be kept empty. Why? Because it is the space for wonder, for possibility, for reaching beyond our grasp; it is the silence without which, in a world of noise, we would never hear the small voice within us that calls out to the eagle-angel above. It is the dark space from which the memory and presence of another truth will slowly rise, like a morning star, to restore the light.

Without these half-felt feelings of emptiness, those whispers from the deep that stir an ache in our soul, a certain dynamic dimension would leave our lives. 'God help any of us,' wrote Ronald Rolheiser, 'if we become so dulled or self-protective, that we are no longer soul-chained to worlds beyond us.' What happens is our need for the security of what we can control outweighs the inner call of transcendence. There is no open threshold over which the Lord Jesus can come. Without that tension between emptiness and fulfilment there's no hope. Eventually we despair.

Few of us are strangers to that despair. But we still keep on trying to trust in this perennial promise of peace, in the creative absence between the 'now' and the 'not yet'. In spite of war, injustice and all kinds of sin, can we believe, as we sing the 'Gloria' with all our hearts this Christmas, that a blossoming of the individual soul, a transformation of our society and planet, is already happening; that this holding together of 'the seen and the unseen', is secure within us?

While we are disturbed at the awesome challenge of our divine destiny, and so often despair at the prospect of either ourselves, or our world, ever getting there, the child, with the seeds of Easter already within him, is a perennial sacrament of both God's immediate vulnerability and eventual invincibility. And, mysteriously, both these mysteries are somehow held together in the present moment.

I like to think that Arthur Clough was waiting in a silent church, fighting his hopelessness, early on a wartime Christmas morning, when he wrote these lines of grace from 'Say Not the Struggle Naught Availeth':

And not by eastern windows only
When daylight comes, comes in the light;
In front, the sun climbs slow, how slowly!
But westward, look, the land is bright!

Shock waves of Bethlehem

It takes some doing to get our heads round the astonishing fact that God stole into our world in the same shape – that of a baby – in which we all started out. The simplicity of it all is almost too much for us. But then, extraordinary things happen in the most ordinary moments.

How we would behave at Mass if we understood its full impact is described by the American writer Annie Dillard in one of her striking reflections. We would strap ourselves to our seats, wear protective headgear, and be attentive to the earth-shaking import of what was happening around us.

We have many ways, she was pointing out, of avoiding what we would rather not face. And so we argue over translations, rubrics and rites. We distract ourselves with the non-essentials, thus escaping the awesome risk of surrendering to the shocking mystery of Incarnation and transubstantiation, of being crucified into the cross-pattern of eucharistic living. But most of all, of grappling with God's unexpected way of becoming present to us.

Something similar happens at Christmas. Eucharist and Incarnation tell the same stunning story about divinity in the most ordinary realities – bread, wine, a baby. The shock waves of the Bethlehem truth still reverberate across the universe – but, as with the Mass, we do not pause to ponder the mystery. We have the experience but we miss the meaning. The profound simplicity of it all is too much for us. We would rather concentrate on something else. And there are many counter-attractions.

But for those who do wish to explore the mystery, how do we get our heads and hearts around the Christian truth that God stole into our world in the same shape as we all started off with? How do we cope with the ensuing belief that the divinity of all of us is now revealed? And how do we make any sense of the consequent expectation that we must therefore embrace our enemies, even die to restore dignity to a dishonoured earth? On such personal decisions and moments depend the salvation of the world.

Mill Hill Missionary Fr Chris told me about the experience of his friend Fr Gerard in a black township in South Africa. The weary parish priest forced himself to attend the last part of a school play during the final week of Advent. This is how he tells the story.

'After the wise men had come and gone I noticed the arrival of three more strange characters – one was dressed in rags, hobbling along with the aid of a stick. The second was naked except for a tattered pair of shorts and was bound in chains. The third was the most weird. He had a whitened face, wore an unkempt grey wig and an Afro shirt.

'As they approached, a chorus of men and women cried out "Close the door, Joseph, they are thieves and vagabonds coming to steal all we have." But Joseph said, "Everyone has a right to this child – the poor, the rich, the unhappy, the untrustworthy. We cannot keep this child for ourselves. Let them enter."

'The men entered and stood staring at the child. Joseph picked up the gifts the wise men had left. To the first strange man he said, "You are poor: take this gold and buy what you need. We will not go hungry." To the second he said, "You are in chains and I don't know how to release you. Take this myrrh – it will heal the wounds on your wrists and ankles." To the third he said, "Your mind is in anguish. I cannot heal you. Maybe the aroma of this frankincense will soothe your troubled soul."

'Then the first man spoke to Joseph. "Do not give me this gift. Anyone who finds me with this gold will think I have stolen it. And sadly, in a few years, this child will end up as a criminal too." The second man said, "Do not give me this ointment. Keep it for the child. One day he will be wearing chains like these." The third man said, "I am lost. I have no faith at all. In the country of my mind there is no God. Let the child keep the incense. He will lose his faith in his Father too."

'While Mary and Joseph covered their faces the three men addressed the child. "Little one, you are not from the land of gold and frankincense. You belong to the country of want and disease. You belong to our world. Let us share our things with you." The first man took off his ragged shirt. "Take these rags. One day you will need them when they tear the garments off your back and you will walk naked."

'The second man said, "When I remove these chains I will put them at your side. One day you will wear them – and then you will really know the pain of humanity." The third man said, "I give you my depression, my loss of faith in God and in everything. I can carry it all no longer. Carry my grief and loss with your own."

'The three men then walked back out into the night. But the darkness was different. Something had happened in the stable. Their blind pain was diminishing. There had been a kind of epiphany. They were noticing the stars now.'

The script of the performance was written by a man from Central Africa. Because his vision was extraordinarily true he told his story well. The unwelcome visitors now knew that God was somehow present in an innocent child who was already destined to be one like them – in all their poverty, pain and sin. And they also began to believe, what we perennially resist, that this human mess was the manger of hope – for themselves and for the world.

Christmas reveals that there is a light within the darkness, a love within the Cross, a life within each death. Our sins and certainties, our wayward compulsions, our despair and desperation, the wars and poverty we collude in – all are redeemed, all are taken care of. And often, it is from precisely there, and maybe only from there, that the redemption of Creation begins. And all because the baby was utterly human.

Above all, Christmas reminds us, as it did the unwelcome visitors, that the most extraordinary things happen in the most ordinary moments. Sr Hilary Lyons, a Missionary Sister of the Holy Rosary working in West Africa, writes about a painting of the Annunciation in Futru parish church in Cameroon. 'Mary is preparing a fire for cooking. Behind her the firewood is stacked. She is turning to add a stick to the fire when a luminous presence surrounds her.' Heavenly intimacy in a human kitchen.

God's secrets are strewn extravagantly around us. God's finger prints are everywhere. Nothing has ever been written by theologians about God's beautiful presence that hasn't been better traced in the crystal calligraphy of a frosty morning. Nothing has ever been preached by saints about divine intimacy that hasn't been better sung by the summer wind in the roadside trees. And nothing has ever been created by artists about incarnate love that hasn't been more poignantly revealed in the sleepy eyes of a new baby.

Light incarnate

A baby contains the mystery of the universe, consecrating all the day-to-day things that sustain us, while every Mass holds and celebrates the divinity of a million galaxies.

In J. D. Salinger's book *Franny and Zooey* there is a scene in which Franny, a 20-year-old theology student, has just come home from college a nervous wreck. Her concerned mother, Bessie, brings her a cup of chicken soup. Franny, unhappy and impatient, pushes the soup away.

Franny's brother Zooey is indignant. 'I'll tell you one thing, Franny,' he says, 'if it's religious life you're studying, you ought to know that you are missing out on every single religious action that's going on in this house. You don't have enough sense to drink a cup of consecrated chicken soup, which is the only kind of chicken soup that Mom ever brings to anybody.'

Zooey saw the kitchen as the church, his mother as a kind of priest, the soup as blessed, the welcome for Franny as God's greeting. Is he right? For the Christian, anything and everything we give in love is consecrated. Since the first Christmas, there is no longer any unconsecrated bread at the family table, no unconsecrated affection between true friends. Since Christmas there is nothing too big or too small in our blessed and broken humanity to be revealed every Sunday as Real Presence.

One day the celebrated violinist Yehudi Menuhin was walking down the corridor of a music academy and came across a young Irish student having his lunch. Not recognising the soda bread sandwich, he asked Liam what he was eating. 'Bread, sir,' the wee lad replied. 'Me ma sent it.'

The great man smiled and was moved to reflect on an Irish mother pouring her love into the dough she was kneading for her beloved son, away from home for the first time. He imagined her baking it, posting it overseas, and homesick Liam slicing it, buttering it – and eating it with great gusto.

Menuhin's imagination was sublimely sacramental and incarnational, yet inspired by something so commonplace – the bread of life wrapped in brown paper, tied with a piece of string and posted in Connemara! In this very ordinary, everyday moment, the musician recognised the love hidden like yeast in the dough, the bread behind the bread, the horizon behind the horizon, the mystery of the whole world in the body of a baby, the unity of everything in God.

Christmas calls us to be God's spies as we penetrate the disguises all around us; to be water-diviners who detect the liquid of life beneath the desert of our days; persistent beachcombers who discover the glimmer of God's gold along the leaden shores of our lives. Without a vibrant sense of incarnate Presence, the human and divine will drift away from each other, and, as W. B. Yeats warned us, all evidence of Incarnation will be erased from the earth.

In an Advent reflection, Symeon the New Theologian (949-1022), saint and mystic, reminds us of that same evidence of God in our own physical bodies too: 'We awaken in Christ's body as Christ awakens our bodies. And everything that is hurt, everything that is shameful, maimed, ugly, irreparably damaged, is in him transformed, recognised as whole, as lovely, and radiant in his light.'

The startling news of Christmas is that Christ is not primarily in the heavens, in the scriptures, in the doctrines of the church, not primarily even in the Eucharist itself. For those who believe that our amazing God became common perishable flesh, Christ is primarily in our own experience, in the ordinariness of our lives and in the silence of our solitude.

In 'Praying', Mary Oliver catches a whisper of the Word that hides in silence:

> It doesn't have to be
> the blue iris, it could be
> weeds in a vacant lot, or a few
> small stones: just
> pay attention, then patch
> a few words together and don't try
> to make them elaborate; this isn't
> a contest but the doorway
> into thanks, and a silence in which
> another voice may speak.

Incarnation is about that other voice – in the silence of the spheres as well as the silence of our souls. Like another Christmas, every Mass, with its fragments of bread and wine, catches and holds a million galaxies and celebrates their divinity on a table. The small crib, the small Host tell the same astonishing story. The mystery of Being itself, the source of life, is named and celebrated as God incarnate in the wonder of Christmas and Eucharist.

'Christmas', John Paul II wrote, 'signifies the taking up into unity with God not only human nature but, in a sense, everything that is flesh … the Incarnation then has a cosmic significance, a cosmic dimension … Even when the Eucharist is celebrated on the small table of a country church it is always celebrated on the altar of the world.'

Orbiting the Moon on Christmas Eve 1968, the crew of *Apollo 8* read the opening chapters of Genesis to a worldwide audience of millions, signing off with 'Merry Christmas, and God bless all of you on the good Earth.'

When negotiating the first human steps on the Moon, Buzz Aldrin brought a blessed wafer with him. 'I ate the tiny Host,' he wrote, 'and swallowed the wine.' One small sip for a human: one giant cosmic celebration for humanity. At this first Christmas Communion in the silence of space we hear, 'You, beloved Sister Moon, are my consecrated Body too.'

After Christmas, nothing is 'merely' natural or ordinary any more. All is now graced. Every human breath is an inspiration of the Holy Spirit; every heartbeat reverberates throughout eternity. We are afraid to believe this astonishing revelation of the divine potential everywhere lest our lives be utterly transformed by it. It is much safer to leave Christmas to the children – and to keep Jesus always a baby.

Every Sunday, the Eucharist repeatedly guarantees what the first Christmas and the first Easter revealed – that every real relationship on earth is sacred; that no bitter tear or heartfelt wish is ever wasted; that no sin is ever left unredeemed; that nothing is lost; that everything, in the end, is harvest.

On the night before Christmas, theologian Karl Rahner hears God whispering to us: 'When you celebrate tomorrow say to me, "You are here. You have come. You have come into everything that exists, into everything that we are." Say only that one thing. That is enough. It is Christmas. Light the candles. They have more right to exist than all the darkness. It is the Christmas that lasts forever.'

And then, in that silent moment, the serious wonder of it strikes us: it is we ourselves, lit from within by the radiance of God, who are called to be those candles of hope, shining incarnate light on a world and a church lost too often in the dark.

Safe haven for the lost

We are all wounded human beings, and the church is there to tell us that it is possible to start over again. But its message of the Saviour is not the preserve of the privileged, it is a beacon of love for all those struggling in the obscurity of sin.

On a dangerous stretch of coast where shipwrecks often occurred, there was once a small lifeboat station. It consisted of just one hut, one boat, a makeshift lighthouse and a few devoted members who kept a constant watch over the sea. Many lives were saved.

The turning point came when the original vision was gradually lost by new and less inspired members. They were unhappy with the poorly equipped hut and the informal atmosphere of the place. They appointed and trained new crew members, and a manual of instruction was drawn up for them, together with a code of dress and behaviour.

Now the lifeboat station became a popular gathering place for its members. They furnished it expensively and began to use it as a sort of club. A huge flagpole replaced the small lighthouse. Fewer members were now interested in risking their lives in times of danger, and the focus of attention became the running of the new club.

About this time, a straying ship was wrecked off the coast and the still-faithful members brought in a boatload of half-drowned people. They were sick and dirty and some of them had black skin, others yellow. These were seen as an unpleasant threat to the spotless new image of the station. An element of fear, exclusion and control crept in.

At the next meeting, there was a severe split among the members. Most of them wanted to stop the club's lifesaving activities as being a hindrance to the normal life of what had now become a privileged institution.

When the church, like the lifeboat station, forgets the original vision, it quickly loses its way. The church exists to reveal the light that protects us when we struggle in the dark. It is there to point the way towards the true shores of our heart, to light our way home. It is there to remind us of who we are and of who we can be.

The church, like Jesus, is meant to measure us at our tallest, to celebrate our divinity from the moment of our birth, to keep our focus on the beckoning horizons of possibility. It traces for us the hidden shape of God in all Creation, the smile of God in all religions, the transforming power of the Holy Spirit in a world called the body of God. The church is there to reveal to us another courageous way of living, a way of believing in the light while it is still dark.

People are waiting to be reassured of this salvation, to be comforted and reconciled within their endless complexities, wounds and restlessness. We are congenitally unfaithful, we are forever tempted, we sin seven times a day. People ache to belong in the inclusive company of those who believe that forgiveness is a non-negotiable way of life.

This is the real universal priesthood. All our hearts are anointed by virtue of the sacrament of birth and baptism. Theologian John O'Donohue sees ordained priesthood as the precious sacrament of the natural and graced priesthood of every human heart. Without this sacramental vision of human holiness at the centre, all around becomes paralysed, disconnected, and falls away. It is happening now.

The Pentecost Spirit is stifled, the gospel is domesticated, the prophet is silenced. There is no wonder any more, or silence, or gentleness. A hardness has set in. Damaged beauty needs a new design – a design that is already traced in the deepest spiritual centre of each member's innermost soul, of each community's commitment to inclusive acceptance and respect.

As a mother holds her child closely while teaching about the hard lessons of life, the church of Jesus is called to be present to us in the same way. We are all failed human beings. Too often we have spoiled what love is, broken our holy vows and damaged precious lives in the process. The church is there to gather us close in our sinfulness, to tell us that it is possible to start all over again, to show us how our pain can be the saving of us. If we are not carefully shown by Mother church how to make our wounds into sacred wounds, we invariably become bitter.

If we are not sensitively drawn to find grace at the heart of our pain, that very heart will go out of us. We long for the tenderness of the fully human Jesus holding and healing us in our hurting, liberating us from the everpresent temptation to despair. There is nothing so like God as being free from fear.

In his poem 'Escape', D. H. Lawrence describes what it is like when we get out of the cages and 'glass bottles' of our own lives, and escape into the forests of freedom:

> Cool, unlying life will rush in,
> and passion will make our bodies taut with power,
> we shall stamp our feet with new power,
> and old things will fall down,
> we shall laugh, and institutions will curl up like burnt paper.

Our image of the God we have preached is too small. So is our understanding of church and of sacraments. The promises of our Saviour were never meant for entitlement for the privileged, or for those who belong to any given institution. They are there as lighthouses for the lost, lifeboat stations for all who are desperate, beacons of pure love for those who are truly poor in their deepest being.

This is the bright message that our people want to hear every Sunday as they prepare for another daunting Monday morning. Loved back into their blessed essence by the community of Jesus, they remake their broken promises.

It is high time for another Pentecost. The Holy Spirit is too surprising, elusive and totally unpredictable to be contained in any institution. Like the wind, she is utterly free – free to sing of a God who has no favourites, who is passionate about our humanity, who forgets our sins and carries to a safe haven every single one of her children.

'So it belongs to us as Christians', Timothy Radcliffe OP said recently in a talk to priests, 'that we rejoice in the very existence of people, with all their fumbling attempts to live and love, whether they are married or divorced or single, whether they are straight or gay, whether their lives are lived in accordance with church teaching or not … The church should be a community in which people discover God's delight in them.'

We are already saved. We do not have to beg for such graces any more. We are all forgiven already for everything. The time and task now is to believe those amazing graces, to thank God for them, and then to heal and empower others by reminding them of their own fragile beauty, yet their immense power.

This is the emerging church we are called to nourish anew. It is starting to blossom from within our hearts and our homes. Its seeds have always been within us.

Leap in the dark

Many of us shy away from the challenge of opening our minds and our hearts to God but unless we can surrender to him fully, we will never complete our final journey.

A late breakfast at home during the holidays. My mother brings in the toast. She tells us the dream she has just woken up from. She dies and goes to heaven, dragging two bulging suitcases labelled 'Good Deeds'. She rings the bell of God's door. No answer. While waiting, she checks her precious baggage, her passport to heaven. The suitcases seem to have grown smaller. Anxiously she presses the bell again. Still no answer. Once more she checks her suitcases. They have now disappeared completely. Utterly distraught, she flees in confusion from the one place she has spent her life trying to reach.

As we piled on the marmalade we discussed the dream. Was it telling our mother that Christian commitment is not about banking up 'good deeds' so as to wrest (yet again) redemption from God? Is it, we wondered, more of a commitment to authenticity? Unhealthy religion can add to our ambivalence. It can hide us from ourselves and from God. Instead of stripping us bare of our veneer of pride to a condition of complete simplicity, the external practice of religion places us in the role of the Scribes – undoubtedly do-gooders, but who were so proud of their good deeds.

Each morning we need to surrender our lives completely into the heart of God. This surrender is of the essence of all great faiths. It is the dark leap. It has a raw and scary quality about it. Even Jesus hesitated. Most of us, too, shy away from such a challenge. Yet without that initial, blind and extreme act of trust, repeated as often as possible every day for as long as we live, all other routine rituals and pastoral performances will only, at best, boost our ego, at worst, poison our soul.

Jesus' words to the Pharisees still chill the hearts of those who are open enough to see and feel the shocking edge of his sharp insight. He hated clerical hypocrisy. In truth, Jesus had little interest in religion at all, or in the trappings of it. His passion was for the utter authenticity of people's lives.

Before embarking on the hard journey of life-long marriage,

of encountering an addiction, of climbing an Everest, the commitment must be total, passionate and non-negotiable. Otherwise the story, and the journey, will be short and sad. There is a costly apprenticeship to discipleship. Thomas Merton once said that he would work with his novices towards achieving surrender only when they stopped slamming doors. There is little point, he felt, in pondering the heights of self-transcendence with those who are not yet aware of the first steps into sensitive living. You begin and end the enterprise by facing a difficult death, by letting go of a very powerful false self.

Some of the 'holiest' powerful personages in our churches have unsurrendered hearts. There is a tenderness that eludes. The whole point of following Jesus is lost. As scripture puts it, they have 'missed the mark'. Most of us are like that. But the few persist in going against the grain of original sin, giving in and giving over to God's unconditional love.

And everyone is equally graced. Surrendered hearts are found among members of all religions and none. To be sure, we need the churches. But the warnings of Jesus must burn in our hearts. The moment the churches begin to believe in themselves more than in the Spirit entrusted to them, believing that they are chosen where others are not, then they are confusing institutional elitism with working for the kingdom.

As another year gets under way, it is so important to reflect on these things. In our anxieties we forget the 'one thing necessary', to enjoy that vibrant sense of freedom through a blessed trusting and a single-minded focus on the divine love in the very centre of our lives. Our in-house preoccupation with liturgical incidentals, and our religious rivalries about who is greatest in the kingdom of heaven, have little to do with a God who just wants to love us, who waits for us to risk returning that love. 'Rake the muck this way, rake the muck that way, it will still be muck,' a Hasidic teaching reminds us. 'In the time you are brooding, you could be on your way, stringing pearls for the delight of heaven.'

'Love and do what you will,' wrote St Augustine. Jesus came to reveal the power of true, human love. The surrender to love will never lead us astray. And the power of that surrender releases the energy of God. St Thérèse of Lisieux never doubted this. She begged to be 'overwhelmed by the flood of God's grace'.

If anyone surrendered and took Jesus at his word it was St Francis, stripped bare of everything, inside and out. There is a drastic finality about the surrender of Mother Teresa, Jean Vanier, Gandhi, to reach, touch and comfort the 'little ones' of the kingdom. And likewise with all the saints we notice around us every day, who quietly surrender their lives in the call of loving service. Whether we are Carmelites living our days and nights in silence, or Princes of the Church spending our time defending the faith, or daily Mass-goers saving our souls, or the millions who never darken the door of a religious institution, it is the same journey for all – the journey of love, the call to surrender, the breaking down of our thinly disguised appetite for power, prestige and possessions, the awareness of our hidden jealousy, petty resentment and ever-so-subtle pride.

Every human saint, religious or not, will have moved beyond the 'pursuit of perfection stage,' the reward/punishment incentive, into another place less limited by flawed motivation and religious constraints. We have to spring the traps of unredeemed religious expectation, where most of us are unknowingly held, before another horizon swings into view. 'Out beyond right and wrong there's a field,' wrote Rumi. 'I'll meet you there.'

Only surrender! 'If you trust the river of life,' wrote Krishnamurti, 'the river of life has an astonishing way of taking care of you.' There can be no other way for us Christians to experience the abundant life before we die; no other way to do God's will; no other way to be broken and refashioned like the surrendered Jesus on the terrible Cross; no other way to flesh again the wonderful Word of truth into our church which, in its necessary human fallibility, is always losing its way.

There is something bold and breathtaking in the vision of Jesus. It is to understand this that we are created. And whatever elitist reasons we may have for our claims to special treatment by the God of truth, without the hard winter of personal and communal surrender, we will never carry the honest light of the summer sun.

We must enter the future fields of freedom not proudly

through guarded gates with our special passes, but humbly, on our knees, in a company of fellow failures, quite unable to believe how, in our sins, we are so undeservedly loved and utterly cherished by a tearful, smiling God. A God who cannot resist the surrendered heart.

Painful but cleansing

The moral authority of the Catholic Church in Ireland has been severely com-
promised by the disclosure of the cover-ups of the widespread abuse of children
by clergy. The revelations indicate a much wider problem which Catholics
must confront head-on if the church is to survive and grow.

Something awful is happening within our Catholic Church. The
recent abuse reports in Ireland offer a stark warning to the
wider church. Bishops are denounced and forced to resign,
archbishops stand accused, dioceses across the world file for bank-
ruptcy, the Vatican itself is held to account. Calls for wide-ranging
diocesan investigations in many countries grow stronger daily.

And yet, apart from those directly involved, there is a strange
silence throughout the church, a kind of detached numbness.
Why is this? In an ecclesiastical system where radical critique is
not welcome, it is often easier to say nothing, or to tell a few white
lies, or not to bother at all. Whether as lay people, priests or bishops, we do not want to be victims of official displeasure, to break
ranks, to be labelled disloyal, awkward or alarmist.

A widespread and silent 'tipping point' in people's faith and
loyalty has been growing for a long time in numerous western
dioceses. The causes of the current malaise are more complicated
than we may wish to explore. As we are seeing in Ireland, the
surface can collapse with a sudden and shocking intensity and
finality. Ireland's disgraceful story today may be told in other
places tomorrow. Many church leaders in European countries
have said as much. Meanwhile, the relentless revelations continue
to erode the moral authority of the church across the world.

But where and when, confused people are asking, will there be a
radical and humble self-examination of the organisation, of its leadership and of its self-awareness as the sacrament of divine love? The
fundamental issue is not only the paedophile phenomenon itself; it
is the structure, culture and flawed theology that leads up to it.

Parishioners ask how a bland 'churchianity' has come to replace a once-vibrant Christianity. There are centuries of reasons.
Many writers, particularly in countries hard hit by various scandals, take certain members of the hierarchy to task. They trace
the desperate efforts of well-intentioned, paternalistic bishops to
ensure damage control by imposed silence lest the 'sins of the

137

sons' be revealed, and Rome be upset. They wonder, too, about the reasons for the continuing silence of the priests and the silence of the laity, given their long-standing difficulties with many of the Vatican's directives and directions.

A transformation within the church will not be facilitated by blame and bitterness, but by a realistic acceptance of the role we all play in its dying and its rising. The clerical model of church authority has drifted too far from the vision of the carpenter's son. Commentators refer to the idolatrous pull of power, privilege and possessions that subtly infect even the most religious organisation when an isolating clericalism replaces a loving servanthood.

Strangely, maybe it is in Ireland, in the midst of its painful and devastating meltdown, and maybe indeed because of it, that elements of the truth may be emerging at last. Lay folk and clergy are beginning to speak out their truth in the public forum even if it brings conflict, shock and anguish within their own ranks and across the country.

Taboos are being broken in the heat of anger. A defensive scapegoating is being revealed. It is painful and hurtful on all sides, but also cleansing. It is shocking and confusing, but healing too. But at least it is authentic and real, and reaching for transparency. Thoughtful lay people are beginning to recognise the subtle sin of mistaking the symbols of religion for the substance of love, the rubric for true worship, external conformity for inner conversion. Many leaders may be astonished at the clear majority-conviction of the faithful about issues such as the need to de-Romanise leadership, the need to relativise false absolutes, the need to recover the radical inclusivity of the gospel.

John Paul II prayed for another 'springtime' for the church. So, too, do anxious people who quietly long for a leadership that will finally say sorry, and then start to learn again from the tender humanity of Jesus. The recovery will be a long season of further conflicts and embarrassing climb-downs.

Beyond the scandals, a radical reform of the whole church – its essential purpose and vision – is urgently needed. And this reformed church will have so much to say to the world. But first it must befriend it. The 'secular' postmodern world is God's body too.

It will all be a vulnerable waiting, a hard lesson, a lot of soul-searching throughout 2010 and way beyond. Richard Rohr OFM and others are exploring the spreading phenomenon of 'the emerging church'. This is not a new organisation for disaffected believers but an ecumenical consensus of those who have redis-covered the charism of contemplation, who, in the spirit of Vatican II, try to distinguish the essentials from the incidentals in church practice and teaching (see www.cacradicalgrace.org).

An emerging church will refuse to build barriers of fearful silence around itself, will distinguish between faith and certainty, will believe in charisma, imagination and joy. People want to be nourished in their precious humanity. They want to be held and supported in the messiness and failures of their precarious lives. They want to be reminded of their beauty, to tell their story, to prophesy with confidence, to have a vision of those bright hori-zons already traced on their hearts by God. Those who still believe are at the edge of the nest waiting to fly.

This green growing will happen only through long, open, difficult and courageous conversations. Maybe a Third Vatican Council is what the Holy Spirit is prompting us to consider. Agendas for it already abound. But first the church must listen so as to be evangelised herself. The voice of the faithful – the *sensus fidelium* – needs to find a forum for a structured response, to find negotiation strategies so as to 'quarrel peacefully', as Cardinal Martini put it.

Like Jesus did, we must hold the tensions and doubts of the church community in our own wounded souls. But there will be no instant reconciliation, nor perfect closure. In 'Healing', D. H. Lawrence wrote:

> ... the wounds to the soul take a long, long time,
> only time can help
> and patience,
> and a certain difficult repentance
> long, difficult repentance,
> realisation of life's mistake,
> and the freeing oneself
> from the endless repetition
> of the mistake
> which mankind at large
> has chosen to sanctify.